Anonymous

Fifty Years' Work of the Hebrew Education Society of Philadelphia

1848-1898

Anonymous

Fifty Years' Work of the Hebrew Education Society of Philadelphia 1848-1898

ISBN/EAN: 9783337318130

Printed in Europe, USA, Canada, Australia, Japan

Cover: Foto ©ninafisch / pixelio.de

More available books at **www.hansebooks.com**

FIFTY YEARS' WORK

OF THE

Hebrew Education Society

OF

Philadelphia.

1848-1898.

PUBLISHED BY THE SOCIETY.

1899.

CONTENTS.

Isaac Leeser.	FRONTISPIECE
First Constitution and By-Laws.	7
Act of Incorporation.	20
Names of First Pupils.	25
First Charity Dinner.	33–37
Second Charity Dinner.	40
Teachers in Hebrew Schools.	45
First Published Annual Report.	47
Maimonides College.	55
Revision of By-Laws.	77
Location of Schools.	84
Young Women's Union.	89
Touro Hall—Tenth and Carpenter Streets	99
Baron de Hirsch Trust.	107
University Extension Lectures.	116
Free Synagogue Service.	119
B'nai B'rith School.	121
Gratz College	123
Legacies	127
Officers of the Society, 1848–1898	130
Officers of the Young Women's Union, 1886–1896	132
Summary.	133

APPENDIX I.

Hebrew School No. 1.	139
Hebrew School No. 2.	140
School No. 3.	141
School No. 4.	141
Sewing School	141
General Night School	144
List of Teachers in Night School and Trade Schools.	145

APPENDIX II.

List of Various Donations	149
Fifty-first Annual Report.	165–194

PREFACE.

The first meeting for the formation of a society whose purpose was the education of Jewish youth in the city of Philadelphia was held on March 7, 1847; on June 4, 1848, a Constitution and By-Laws were adopted, and on July 16th the first regular meeting of the Society took place.

At the annual meeting of the Society, held March 13, 1898, it was decided to commemorate the close of the first half-century of the existence of the Society by the publication of a memorial volume.

A brief but comprehensive history of the inception and growth of the Society is accordingly presented in the following pages, compiled almost exclusively from its official records.

In this review of a half century of active communal effort, the life work of Isaac Leeser stands out as a landmark in the history of the Jewish educational movement which is so marked a feature of our present time. It was Isaac Leeser who brought the Hebrew Education Society into existence, and it has been the spirit with which he imbued the organization that has enabled it to overcome the obstacles which for a decade after his death beset its way. To him, furthermore, was due the early effort towards a higher education which took form in the Maimonides College, and, in order to make the record of that worthy undertaking more accessible to students of this subject, its plan, as embodied by its rules and regulations, has been printed in full.

Since 1851, when the first Hebrew School of the Society was established on Zane street, the development of its work has steadily proceeded, increasing in breadth and scope with the growing needs of the Jewish community of Philadelphia. The Hebrew school originally instituted has been continued, with various changes of location, in the central district of the city, and two others have been established and maintained at outlying locations. To these have been added a number of English night schools, and industrial schools.

The policy pursued by the management during the last twenty years was not changed from former methods because of a desire to have something new, but for the reason that the public had evinced a positive disinclination to continue the support of the school as it was then conducted.

In the pursuance of its general objects, the present policy of the Society, as definitely laid down in its official declarations, may here be quoted as follows:

"To keep the expenditures within the income."

"To allow the use of any available portion of the Society's buildings for charitable or educational purposes generally, free of charge."

"Teachers to speak English without a foreign accent; preference to be given those studying for a profession or pursuing courses at a university for a general education."

"English teachers to be High School graduates."

The men and women of Philadelphia who have contributed their means to the Society, may feel content with the thought that it has been applied to the highest of philanthropic work—the instruction and uplifting of the children of their people.

The future holds greater possibilities than the past afforded. The community is awakening, still too slowly, to the import of these possibilities, and to the fact that the most far-reaching philanthropy consists in intellectual and moral education which renders the recipient self-reliant and self-sustaining.

Let us hope that a kind Providence, which has implanted in the hearts of the Members, Friends and Managers of the Hebrew Education Society the desire to maintain its good work, and which has watched over and supported them during the last half century, will guide and direct them in the future, and instil in the hearts of their descendants and successors that love for Judaism, its culture and its history, which can alone perpetuate our religion and deliver it in its purity to our posterity.

HISTORICAL REVIEW.

The Hebrew Education Society

FIFTY YEARS' WORK.

The foundation of an institution for the education of the Jewish youth was early agitated in Philadelphia. At the beginning of the second quarter of the present century German Jews were coming to this city in great numbers, and they proceeded at once to establish a synagogue and charitable societies. The native-born Jewish population was rapidly becoming greater and it was recognized generally that something had to be done in order to educate fittingly the younger generation in the precepts of their fathers, and in a manner that would best equip them to cope with the exigencies of American life.

There were, it is true, Hebrew teachers in the city, but they were not adequate to the needs of the community. The compensation paid to these private tutors was very small, and it did not encourage many of them to pursue their labors. Good text-books were few and these were strongly tinctured with Christian theology. The idea of a college, in which children born of Jewish parents could be instructed in English and in the classics, in the liberal arts and in the Hebrew language and literature, had long been in a nascent condition, and it was soon felt by the members of the Jewish community in Philadelphia that such a college was an urgent and ever-increasing necessity.

Already prior to 1840, Mordecai M. Noah, the famous traveler, consul-general, play-wright, journalist and politician, turned his attention to a plan for the formation of a Hebrew College in the United States. Later, he wrote, under date of

August 18, 1843, an open letter on this subject to the Rev. Isaac Leeser, which was published in the September number of

SOLOMON GANS
Charter Member
Board of Officers, 1855—1856
Trustee Maimonides College

the first volume of *The Occident*. There Major Noah sketched in brief outline his plan for the formation of a Hebrew seminary, " where children of the Jewish faith can obtain a classical education and at the same time be properly instructed in the Hebrew language, where they can live in conformity to our laws and acquire a liberal knowledge of the principles of their religion."

Isaac Leeser, in a prefatory note to Major Noah's letter, warmly commended the plan and invited every one interested in the cause of education to co-operate with him and to give " the subject the serious reflection which it deserves." No one recognized the need of such an institution more than Isaac Leeser. His magazine, *The Occident*, became the organ of the new movement, and he advocated it whenever a happy occasion offered itself. Isaac Leeser contributed more than any other man to the establishment of the Hebrew Education Society of Philadelphia.

A year after the appearance in print of Noah's letter, the Rev. I. Felsenheld communicated to *The Occident*, (Vol. II., p. 249) a plan which, in the opinion of its author, would speedily effect a solution of the problem. He proposed to teach in the school Hebrew grammar,

MOSES NATHANS
Charter Member
Board of Officers, 1848—1852
1860—1861

Catechism, Latin, Greek, English grammar, mathematics, geography, history, German and French. He further proposed that he himself should conduct it and give instruction in most of the branches in his curriculum. As soon as twenty pupils would be procured he would open the school at the "earliest possible day." This plan never matured, and the Rev. Isaac Leeser continued to moot the subject through the columns of *The Occident*, although little success had as yet attended his efforts.

SOLOMON ISAACS
Charter Member

Towards the close of 1846 interest in the project revived and steps were taken to secure enough money to carry the plan to a successful issue. On January 27, 1847, a ball was given in the old Chinese Museum, under the management of Michael H. De Young, Solomon Gans, Moses Nathans, Isaac Nathans, Solomon Isaacs, R. Benjamin, H. Pincus, Simon M. Klasser, Lazarus Schloss, Michael Moyer, David Van Biel and Herman Weiler. It was known as the Hebrew School Fund Ball, and it was given for the especial purpose of raising funds for the "establishment of a Hebrew School in this city." The receipts netted over three hundred dollars, and this money went into a depository known as the Hebrew School Fund.

About a month after the ball, a public call was issued in the newspapers to all Israelites, to meet and receive the report of the Trustees of the Hebrew School Fund Ball, and to adopt such measures "as will further the ends of this laudable object." On March 7, 1847, in pursuance of this

MICHAEL MOYER
Board of Officers, 1864-1865

call, twenty-five gentlemen met and proceeded to consider the disposition of the money. The Rev. Isaac Leeser called the meeting to order. Zadoc A. Davis was elected chairman and S. M. Klasser secretary. M. H. De Young, the chairman of the Fund, reported that the net proceeds of the ball amounted to $312, of which $300 was deposited with the Pennsylvania Life Annuity Company, in the names of M. H. De Young, Moses Nathans and Joseph Levi, as trustees of the Hebrew School Fund Ball. On motion of Abraham Hart it was carried unanimously, that the name of Simon Elfeit be added to the Trustees. On motion it was resolved that a committee of seven be appointed with power to collect donations and yearly subscriptions to further the object of the "establishment of a Hebrew and English school." It was further resolved that as soon as $2,000 will have accumulated, a general meeting shall be held in which the most advantageous disposal of the money would be duly considered. A subscription list was opened at the close of the meeting, and a number of the gentlemen

ABRAHAM HART
Charter Member
Treasurer, 1848—1875
Board of Officers, 1876—1881
Trustee Maimonides College

present subscribed their names to various sums amounting to nearly $450.

HYMAN POLOCK
Charter Member
Board of Officers, 1848—1862

On March 19, 1848, a general meeting of the subscribers to the Fund was held in the vestry room of the Synagogue Mickvé Israel, then on Cherry Street. Abraham Hart was elected Treasurer. It was stated that a second ball in aid of the Fund had been given, and it was as brilliant a success as the first one. As a result $427.15 had been invested in the names of the Trustees. Simon Elicit having declined to serve as a member of the Board of Trustees, and as the meeting had resolved upon two additional members, Julius Stern and L. H. Blum were duly appointed. It is interesting to note that as the funds were deposited with the Pennsylvania Company, Hyman Gratz, the president, was notified of the appointment of the additional members.

At the next meeting, the Rev. Isaac Leeser, after dwelling upon the necessity and the benefits of a Hebrew education for Jewish children, called up a resolution which was unanimously adopted. It provided "that a committee of three persons (afterwards increased to seven) be appointed to draft a constitution and by-laws for the formation of a Hebrew Education Society." Agreeable to this resolution the chair appointed as the committee, the Rev. Isaac Leeser, Hyman Polock, L. Bomeisler, Julius Stern, Abraham S.

MARCUS CAUFFMAN
Charter Member
Board of Officers, 1848—1856

Wolf, Joseph M. Asch and Simon Elfelt. A committee was also appointed to prepare printed circulars and distribute them to all Jewish families.

On June 4, the Constitution and By-Laws having been unanimously adopted, the chair was authorized to call a meeting for the organization of the Society and the election of officers.

On July 16, 1848, the Hebrew Education Society was formally organized. Zadoc A. Davis, who had acted as chairman of all the previous meetings, was unable to be present owing to absence from the city, and Solomon Solis served in his stead.

Following is a copy of the Constitution and By-Laws adopted on June 4, and which was formally signed by the members on July 16, 1848:

ABRAHAM S. WOLF
Charter Member
Board of Officers, 1848–1849
Vice-President, 1849–1854
President, 1854–1862
Board of Officers, 1862–1876

CONSTITUTION
AND
BY-LAWS
OF THE
HEBREW EDUCATION SOCIETY OF PHILADELPHIA.

ADOPTED AT A TOWN MEETING OF ISRAELITES

ON SUNDAY, SIVAN 3, 5608, JUNE 4, 1848.

PHILADELPHIA:
C. SHERMAN, PRINTER.
5608.

OFFICERS FOR THE FIRST YEAR.

President,
SOLOMON SOLIS.

Vice-President,
SIMON ELFELT.

Treasurer,
ABRAHAM HART.

Secretary,
MOSES A. DROPSIE.

Assistant Secretary,
SIMON M. KLASSER.

Managers.

Isidore Binswanger,	Moses Nathans,
Solomon N. Carvalho,	Joseph Newhouse,
Marcus Cauffman,	Hyman Polock,
Lewis J. Cohen,	Julius Cohen,
Jacob Langsdorf,	Herman Van Beil,
Isaac Leeser.	Abraham S. Wolf.

School Directors,
M. A. Dropsie, A. Hart, I. Leeser, S. Solis, A. S. Wolf.

Trustees,
Mayer Arnold, Mos. Nathans, Jos. Schoneman.

PREAMBLE.

Penetrated with the conviction of the necessity of a thorough religious education of all Israelites, and in view of the absence of proper schools where the same can be imparted; we the subscribers have associated ourselves for the purpose of raising funds, and to effect therewith the establishment of such schools, as will enable all Israelites of this city and county, to receive instruction in religion, the Hebrew and the English languages, the usual branches of education, and all such other subjects as the circumstances of the funds and the capacity of the scholars may enable the directors to afford.

CONSTITUTION.

ARTICLE I.

SECT. 1. The name of the Society shall be "THE HEBREW EDUCATION SOCIETY OF PHILADELPHIA." חברת חנוך נערים

ARTICLE II.

SECT. 1. Every member shall pay three dollars per annum, in such manner as may be fixed by the by-laws.

SECT. 2. Any male Israelite of twenty-one years of age, may apply to any meeting of the Board to be elected a member, and if he receives a majority of the votes of the Board present at the next stated meeting of the Board, he shall be a member of this Society. It is, however, provided, that the Board may postpone the election of any applicant to a future meeting if they deem it proper.

SECT. 3. No member one year in arrears shall be

allowed to vote or hold office, unless previously liberated from his dues by the Board of Officers.

SECT. 4. Every member after his election, shall sign the Constitution before he shall be entitled to vote.

ARTICLE III.

SECT. 1. The officers of this Society shall be one President, one Vice-President, one Treasurer, one Secretary, one Assistant Secretary, and twelve Directors, who shall constitute the Board of Managers, and hold their respective offices for one year, or till their successors shall have been chosen, in case no election shall be held at the regular day for elections.

SECT. 2. The annual election shall hereafter be held on the Sunday before Shebuoth.

SECT. 3. The Board shall meet four times every year, or oftener if required by the President, or three members of the Board; the first meeting every year shall be held three weeks after the annual election, and quarterly thereafter; and at the first meeting of the Board, they shall elect the School Directors, to serve for one year.

SECT. 4. There shall be elected by and from the Board of Managers, five School Directors, who shall meet monthly, and have the superintendence of the school or schools to be established, and report their proceedings to the quarterly meeting of the Board of Managers.

SECT. 5. All vacancies are to be filled by the Board of Managers.

ARTICLE IV.

SECT. 1. The President shall preside at all meetings of the Society and Board, and in his absence the Vice-President; and in the absence of both, the meeting shall appoint a chairman.

SECT. 2. After the accounts shall have been passed by the Board, the President shall draw his warrant on the Treasurer, from a printed order-book (with a cheque marging, without which no money shall be drawn from the treasury. Provided always, that he may draw for any account not exceeding ten dollars, without first laying the same before the Board.

Sect. 3. In his absence, or sickness, the Vice-President (or other presiding officer), shall have the same power.

Sect. 4. He shall have power to convene meetings of the Society, Board of Managers, and School Directors, whenever he may deem it necessary.

Sect. 5. Whenever ten members address a written application to the President, stating the object of the call, he shall forthwith convene a general meeting for not later than ten days after the requisition has been presented to him.

ARTICLE V.

Sect. 1. The Treasurer shall take charge of all the moneys and securities of the Society, and he shall credit every member, donor, or contributor, with his or her contribution.

Sect. 2. He shall pay all orders duly signed by the President or other presiding officer.

Sect. 3. He shall keep a regular account of all sums received and paid by him, and furnish a statement of the funds in his hands at every meeting of the Board, and a general statement to the yearly meeting of the Society.

Sect. 4. He shall give such security for the faithful performance of his duties, as shall be approved of by the Board of Managers.

Sect. 5. He shall deliver all moneys, papers, and accounts, and all other property of whatsoever kind, belonging to this Society, to his successor in office, within two weeks after the election of said successor, on being duly notified by the President, or other presiding officer.

ARTICLE VI.

Sect. 1. The Secretary shall attend all general and

Board meetings, and shall keep fair and correct minutes of all transactions of said meetings.

SECT. 2. He shall make out all bills, and hand them over to the Treasurer for collection.

SECT. 3. The Assistant Secretary shall make out all notices for meetings, and attend the meetings of the School Directors, keep the minutes of their transactions, and perform all the duties of the Secretary in his absence.

ARTICLE VII.

THE SCHOOL.

SECT. 1. As soon as the funds in hand, and the subscription of the members will warrant the undertaking, a school or schools, for both males and females, shall be established, in which are to be taught in the first instance Hebrew, according to both the German and Portuguese reading, Religion, and the elementary branches of an English education, the higher branches to be added as the scholars progress, and the funds will permit.

SECT. 2. The school shall be placed under the direction of the five School Directors, who shall receive all applications for admission into the school, and no scholar shall be admitted without a written order of said Directors.

SECT. 3. The Board of Managers shall have the power to fix annually the amount which each pay scholar shall have to pay for tuition.

SECT. 4. The School Directors shall admit all applicants (provided of good character) at the price affixed by the Board of Managers, if the application is signed by the parent or guardian, and states that the scholar is to be a pay scholar; and should the parent or guardian desire the scholars admitted as non-paying ones, they are to receive them as such.

SECT. 5. The Board of Managers shall have the power to elect the teachers after application of the candidates shall have been made to, and they have been recommended by the School Directors.

SECT. 6. The teachers' salaries shall be paid by the Board of Managers.

SECT. 7. The number of teachers shall be determined every year by the Board of Managers, according to the circumstances of the Society, and the wants of the scholars.

SECT. 8. The salaries of the teachers shall be paid quarterly, after having been passed on by the Board of Managers, and the orders being duly signed by the President or other presiding officer.

SECT. 9. The Chairman of the School Directors shall be ex-officio President of the school or schools to be established by this Society.

SECT. 10. The branches of education shall be determined from time to time by the Board of Managers.

SECT. 11. The School Directors shall have power to form a code of laws for the government of the school, to be submitted for approval to the Board of Managers.

SECT. 12. The choice of books, &c., and the giving of premiums, as also the formation of a school library, are to be left to the School Directors.

SECT. 13. The location of the school or schools to be established by this Society, is to be left to the Board of Managers.

ARTICLE VIII.

SECT. 1. The Society shall elect three Trustees, in whose names the stocks, funds, and property of the Society shall be vested, and whenever the Society shall be incorporated, they shall transfer all the said stocks, funds, and property belonging to the Society, to the corporation.

ARTICLE IX.

SECT. 1. All elections for officers shall be by written ballot.

ARTICLE X.

Sect. 1. This Constitution shall not be altered, repealed or amended, except the proposition shall have been made at one general meeting and passed on by the votes of two-thirds of the members present, at a subsequent general meeting, provided the amendment has been inserted in the notice of the meeting.

ARTICLE XI.

Sect. 1. This Society shall not be dissolved while there are five members, and when this shall be the case, the remaining members shall place the funds in some public securities, to be held by three trustees in trust, for purposes of education, as contemplated by this Constitution, and transferred to any other Society which may hereafter be formed on a similar plan, and for similar purposes, in the City and County of Philadelphia; the Trustees are to be empowered to pay over the annual interest for the education of Hebrew children for the purposes herein mentioned.

ARTICLE XII.

Sect. 1. The Society shall have power to pass all regulations and by-laws, not repugnant to this Constitution, the Jewish laws, and the Constitution and laws of the United States and the State of Pennsylvania.

ARTICLE XIII.

Sect. 1. Any officer or member may be expelled, or otherwise dealt with, by the Society, on an impeachment, provided such impeachment is signed by at least four members, and a copy of the same, with the notice of time and place of meeting, be furnished the accused, at least one week previously. Two-thirds of the members of the Society present at any such meeting shall determine the guilt or innoence of the accused; provided, always, that the Board may suspend any member of the Board under the above regulations, subject to an appeal to the Society.

BY-LAWS.

SECT. 1. Half an hour after the time specified in the notices for calling the meeting, the President or other presiding officer, shall take the chair. The order of business shall be as follows:—

I. The roll shall be called.

II. The minutes of the preceding meeting shall be read and approved of, or amended if any error have been committed.

III. Election of officers shall take place.

IV. Communications to the Society shall be read.

V. Reports of committees shall be read.

VI. Business laid over from a former meeting shall be attended to.

VII. New business shall then be introduced.

SECT. 2. No motion shall be received unless it is seconded; and if requested by the chair, it is to be reduced to writing. Every motion is to be stated from the chair before debate shall be had thereon; and until it shall be decided, no other shall be received, except to amend or postpone the original motion, or a motion to adjourn, which shall always be in order, and be decided without debate; and no motion to reconsider shall be received unless the mover and seconder have voted with the majority. Questions of filling up blanks shall be taken first on the highest number; and no member shall speak more than twice upon any question, unless permitted by the chair.

SECT. 3. The yeas and nays shall be taken, if required

by four members of the Society or two of the Board, and entered on the minutes.

Sect. 4. The presiding officer shall appoint all committees, unless otherwise ordered by the Society, and may vote on the following subjects:—the revision of the constitution or by-laws, and expulsion of a member; but in no other case, except when the meeting is equally divided, when he shall have the casting vote.

Sect. 5. Thirteen members shall form a quorum of the Society, and four of the Board and three School Directors shall form a quorum for the transaction of all business.

Sect. 6. If the Treasurer is compelled to be absent from town for more than two weeks, he is to place the funds of the Society in the hands of the Vice-President, who is then to act as treasurer *pro tem*.

Sect. 7. The Board, if deemed requisite, may employ a suitable person to deliver the notices for the meetings of the Society or Board, and to act as collector, and allow him a compensation for his services.

Sect. 8. The following fines shall be enforced:—A member refusing to act as President, when elected, shall be fined $5.00; Vice-President, Secretary, or Treasurer, $3.00; a member of the Board, or School Director, $1.50. A member behaving disorderly at any meeting, not exceeding (at the option of the presiding officer), 50 dollars; provided always, that a person who has served two years, shall not be fined for refusing to hold office for a space of three years after the expiration of his second term; and provided an appeal may always be had to the Society.

Sect. 9. Any member not paying his annual subscription for two years, or refusing to pay his fines, may be expelled by the Board, unless excused by the Society.

Sect. 10. Every member at a meeting shall vote upon all questions, unless excused by the Society or Board, as the case may be.

Sect. 11. Collections are to be made quarterly.

Sect. 12. No alteration, amendment, or addition to these

by-laws shall be made, unless proposed at one meeting of the Board or Society, and confirmed at the next meeting of the Society, by a vote of two-thirds of all the members present.

LIST OF MEMBERS.

Lewis M. Allen,
Mayer Arnold,
David Barnet,
A. I. H. Bernal,
Isidore Binswanger,
Solomon N. Carvalho,
Marcus Cauffman,
Lewis J. Cohen,
Myer D. Cohen,
Julius Davidson,
Zadok A. Davis,
Henry De Boer,
Moses A. Dropsie,
Solomon Eckstein,
Simon Elfelt,
Wm. Florance,
P. Friedenberg,
J. Geissenberger,
M. Gerstly,
Abraham Hart,
Selig Hohenfels,
Aaron Isaacs,
Solomon Isaacs,
Julius Jacob,
Israel Jacob,

Alfred T. Jones,
Simon M. Klasser,
B. Klein,
Jacob Langsdorf,
Isaac Leeser,
David Levin,
Moses Nathans,
N. E. Nelson,
Joseph Newhouse,
George Phillips,
Hyman Polock,
Michael Reinhard,
Joseph Schoneman,
M. Seidenbach,
David H. Solis,
Solomon Solis,
Julius Stern,
L. Sulzberger,
David Van Beil,
Herman Van Beil,
Moses Vanderslice,
Abraham S. Wolf,
Abraham Wolff,
Samuel Wohl, M. D.,
Isaac Yassner.

The first officers of the Society were elected at this meeting: Solomon Solis, President; Simon Elfelt, Vice-President; Abraham Hart, Treasurer; Zadoc A. Davis, Secretary, and S. M. Klasser, Assistant Secretary. The first Board of Directors were: Abraham S. Wolf, Hyman Polock, Moses A. Dropsie, Marcus Cauffman, Julius Stern, Joseph Newhouse, Moses Nathans, Jacob Langsdorf, H. Van Beil, Isaac Leeser, Lewis J. Cohen and Alfred T. Jones. Three trustees to take charge of the old Hebrew School Fund were Moses Nathans, Mayer Arnold and Joseph Schoneman. They were instructed by resolution to apply to the five trustees, the guardians of the money "collected for the purpose of promoting education among Israelites of Philadelphia," and to receive the funds which had been deposited by them with the Pennsylvania Company. At a subsequent meeting Moses A. Dropsie was elected secretary in place of Zadoc A. Davis, who had declined to serve, and Isidore Binswanger and Solomon N. Carvalho were added to the Board of Directors, owing to the resignation of Alfred T. Jones and to the election of Mr. Dropsie.

SOLOMON SOLIS
Charter Member
First President, 1848 — Died, 1854

A curriculum and rules for the government of the school were drawn up by a committee, of which the Rev. Isaac Leeser was chairman. There were to be seven classes, and the syllabus of instruction reminds one as befitting a college more than a school. "English and Hebrew spelling and reading," were to be taught to the first class, while the more advanced pupils were to be instructed in "geometry, natural history, natural philosophy, Rabbinical literature, French, German, Latin, Greek, botany and chemistry."

The Rev. Isaac Leeser, Abraham S. Wolf and Abraham Hart were appointed a committee to petition the state legislature for a charter, and on April 7, 1849, "An Act to Incorporate the Hebrew Education Society," received the sanction of the Governor. In addition to the preparatory schools, the Society was authorized by its charter to establish a college, with power to confer degrees.

MOSES A. DROPSIE
Charter Member
Secretary, 1848—1849   Board of Officers, 1849—1861
Vice President, 1861—1862   President, 1862—1870
Board of Officers, 1870—1871   Board of Officers, 1874—1877
President, 1880—1892   Life Member of Board of Officers
President Maimonides College

Following is a copy of the Charter approved April 7, 1849, and also the Supplementary Act approved April 11, 1866:

AN ACT

TO INCORPORATE THE HEBREW EDUCATION SOCIETY OF PHILADELPHIA.

SECTION 1. *Be it enacted by the Senate and House of Representatives of the Commonwealth of Pennsylvania, in General Assembly met, and it is hereby enacted by the authority of the same,* That Solomon Solis, Simon Elfelt, Abraham Hart, Moses A. Dropsie, Solomon N. Carvalho, Isidore Binswanger, Marcus Cauffman, Lewis J. Cohen, Simon M. Klosser, Jacob Langsdorf, Isaac Leeser, Moses Nathans, Joseph Newhouse, Hyman Polock, Julius Stern, Herman Van Beil, Abraham S. Wolf, Lewis M. Allen, Mayer Arnold, Simon W. Arnold, David Barnett, Leon Berg, A. I. H. Bernal, Bernard Blum, Myer D. Cohen, Julius Davidson, Zadoc A. Davis, Henry De Boer, Solomon Eckstein, David Eger, William Florance, P. Friedenberg, Solomon Gans, J. Geisenberg, M. Gerstley, Jacob Gumpel, Selig Hohenfels, Aaron Isaacs, Solomon Isaacs, Julius Jacobs, Israel Jacobs, B. Klein, Henry Lazarus, David Levine, N. E. Nelson, Joseph A. Levy, George Phillips, Michael Reinhard, Joseph Schoneman, M. Seidenbach, Henry Simson, David H. Solis, Mayer Sternberger, L. Sulzberger, David Van Beil, Simon Sternberger, Moses Vanderslice, Abraham Wolff, Isaac Tassner and Doctor Samuel Wolff, and all and every other person or persons who shall hereafter become members of the Hebrew Education Society of Philadelphia, be and are hereby created and made a corporation or body politic and corporate by the name and style of "THE HEBREW EDUCATION SOCIETY OF PHILADELPHIA," and by that name shall have perpetual succession, and be capable in law to take, hold and dispose of estates, real and personal whatsoever, and to sue and be sued, and to receive and make all deeds, transfers, contracts, conveyances and covenants whatsoever, and to make, have and use a common seal, and the same to change and renew at pleasure, and generally to do every other act or thing necessary to carry into effect the provisions of this act, and promote the objects and designs of said corporation.

SEC. 2. The object and design of the said corporation shall be the establishment of a school or schools within the limits of the city and county of Philadelphia, in which are to be taught the elementary branches of education, together with the sciences, and modern and ancient languages, always in combination with instruction in Hebrew language, literature and religion, in the manner that may be determined, from time to time, by the proper officers of the Society, and as the same may be set forth in their Constitution and By-Laws and School Regulations; *Provided*, said Constitution, By-Laws and Regulations are not inconsistent with this charter, or with the Constitution of the United States, or the Constitution and Laws of this Commonwealth.

SEC. 3. It shall also be lawful for the said corporation to establish, whenever their funds will permit the same to be done, a superior seminary of learning within the limits of this Commonwealth, the faculty of which seminary shall have power to furnish to graduates and others the usual degrees of Bachelor of Arts, Master of Arts, and Doctor of Law and Divinity, as the same is exercised by other colleges established in this Commonwealth.

SEC. 4. The Society shall have power to adopt a Constitution and make By-Laws, and the same to amend, alter or repeal at pleasure.

SEC. 5. The said Society shall not at any time have, hold, enjoy or receive a clear yearly income exceeding twelve thousand dollars, without first obtaining authority from the Legislature of this Commonwealth.

SEC. 5. The Legislature shall have power at any time, when the privileges hereby granted shall appear injurious to the public, to repeal, alter or amend this act; but no such repeal, alteration or amendment shall affect any engagement to which the said corporation shall have become a party previous thereto; and in case of such repeal the said corporation shall have a reasonable time to bring their accounts to a final settlement and termination.

     (Signed) WILLIAM F. PACKER,
        Speaker of the House of Representatives.
     (Signed) GEORGE DARSIE,
        Speaker of the Senate.

APPROVED—The seventh day of April, one thousand eight hundred and forty-nine (1849).

     (Signed) WM. F. JOHNSON.

An Act supplementary to an Act to incorporate the Hebrew Education Society of Philadelphia, approved April seventh, one thousand eight hundred and forty-nine (1849).

SECTION 1. Be it enacted by the Senate and House of Representatives of the Commonwealth of Pennsylvania in General Assembly met, and it is hereby enacted by the authority of the same, that the pupils of the school or schools of the Hebrew Education Society possessing the qualifications prescribed for the admission of pupils into the boys' and girls' high schools of the City of Philadelphia, shall be admitted to the said boys' and girls' high schools without any previous attendance in the public schools of the First School District.

     (Signed) JAMES R. KELLEY,
        Speaker of the House of Representatives.
     (Signed) DAVID FLEMING,
        Speaker of the Senate.

APPROVED—The eleventh day of April, one thousand eight hundred and sixty-six (1866).

     (Signed) A. G. CURTIN.

At the meeting May 13, 1866, the following vote of thanks was recorded:

"*Resolved*, that the thanks of the Society be given to James Freeborn, Esq., for his faithful services in procuring the supplement to the Act incorporating this Society."

An event of unusual interest in the history of the Jews of Philadelphia, was the opening of the first school of the Society, on Monday, April 7, 1851. The hall of the old Phœnix Hose Company on Filbert (then Zane) street between Seventh and Eighth streets, had been selected by the Board of School Directors, and comfortable rooms were fitted up for the reception of the pupils. The Hebrew Sunday-School, the oldest Jewish Sunday-school in America, then occupied part of the same building. It had been in existence thirteen years. On Sunday, April 6, 1851, the Rev. Isaac Leeser delivered the opening address, in which he emphasized the importance of Hebrew education and the great good about to be accomplished.

ISIDORE BINSWANGER
Charter Member
Board of Officers, 1848—1870
President, 1876—1878
Board of Officers, 1878—1880
Trustee Maimonides College

"You never, we trust," he said, "will regret the exertions and outlay you have made in this cause;"—and we all know to-day that his words rang true.

The next day the school was opened, twenty-two pupils being present. Rich and poor freely mingled, and no one, except the Board of School Directors, knew who were pay-scholars and who were not. Michael M. Allen was the first instructor in Hebrew, and Miss Evelyn Bomeisler taught the English branches. Seven weeks after the opening of the school the number of pupils had increased to seventy-one, and an additional corps of instructors was found to be necessary. Miss Anna Murray and Miss Clara Weil (who subsequently became the wife of the Rev. Dr. Sabato Morais), were elected assistant teachers. The school, under the skillful direction of its teacher and of the Board of School Directors, prospered from the start; the attendance increased, the donations became larger, a greater interest was manifested in its work. The Mickvé Israel Congregation appropriated two hundred dollars, and the members of the Congregation Rodef Shalom asked that a new school be started in a part of the city more accessible to German residents. In this connection it may be of interest to many of the friends of the Society to recall to their minds the names of those who were the first pupils of the school, and at the same time show that the neighborhoods where Jews formerly resided were, in a measure, again occupied by later arrivals.

MISS EVELYN BOMEISLER
First English Teacher

JACOB GUMPEL
Charter Member

On March 19, 1851, "the following names of scholars were given in:" Emanuel Goldstein, 8 Crown street; Julia Lieber, Race, between 9th and 10th; Cecelia Eger, 36 Wood street; Frances Eger, 36 Wood street; Hyman Newhouse, 35 Marshall street; Henry Clay Newhouse, 35 Marshall street. On March 30th: Jacob S. Cohen, 86 N. 7th; Leon Cohen, 86 N. 7th; Matilda Levy, 185 South street; Julia Gumpel, Hannah Gumpel, Samuel

HEBREW EDUCATION SOCIETY. 25

Gumpel, Dianna Gumpel, Moses Gumpel, Buttonwood street above 10th, next to the public school, south side; Caroline Spatz; Benjamin Bloomingdale, 5th below Willow; L. G. Bloomingdale, 5th below Willow; Theodore Pottsdamer, Lewis Pottsdamer, 6 Brown's Court, Newmarket below Coates.

DR. AARON S. BETTELHEIM
Prof. Maimonides College
(Mishna and Shulchan Aruch)
Board of Officers, 1867-1869

On April 7th, the following names were received: Jacob Hyneman, 22 S. 3d street; Augustus Hyneman, 22 S. 3d street; Ansel Homberg, 17 Cherry street; Moses Homberg, 17 Cherry street; Isaac Homberg, 17 Cherry street; Abraham Eckstein, 12 Wood street; Abraham Lipman, 222½ South street; Louisa Lipman, 222½ South street; Charity S. Ritterband, 86 Arch street; Anne Hyneman, 3d above Tammany; Rachael Hyneman, 3d above Tammany; Barton Hyneman, 3d above Tammany. From this time on until May 12th, the following: Henry M. Davis, 365 South street; Hannah Stein, Brown's Court, Franklin near Coates; Emma Rosenberg, Newmarket and Green; Edward Goldman, North street, between 10th and 11th, above Race; Julia Arnold, 5th and Noble; Alice Arnold, 5th and Noble; Benjamin Baer, McCloud's Court, 4th and Race; Rebecca Baer, McCloud's Court, 4th and Race; Leah Jacob, South, between 7th and 8th; Isabella Jacob, South, between 7th and 8th; Israel Jacob, South, between 7th and 8th; M. Croneberg, Vernon street; Miriam Marcusé, 494 Market street;

CHARLES BLOOMINGDALE
Board of Officers, 1846-1860
Trustee Maimonides College

Pina Marcusé, 494 Market street; Jette Marcusé, 494 Market street; I. H. Harvey, 3d below South; Frances Harvey, 3d below South; Eleazer Marcus, 260 S. 6th street; Caroline Marcus, 260 S. 6th street; Clara Levi, 209 S. 6th street; Israel Levi, 209 S. 6th street; Theodore Mayer, 4th near Arch; Michael Gothelf, 250 South street; Clara Gothelf, 250 South street; Fanny Gothelf, 250 South street; Anna Fulda, South, between 6th and 7th; Abraham Roggenberger, Coates near 2d; Caroline Pragheimer, 150 N. Front; S. Pragheimer, 150 N. Front; Isaac Lang, 298 N. 10th; Ansel Lang, 298 N. 10th; Orlando Nathans, Judith Nathans, Helen Nathans, Cornelius Nathans, Chestnut st., near 20th."

Hon. MAYER SULZBERGER
Board of Officers, 1866—1880
Vice-President, 1880—1884
Hebrew Teacher
Trustee Maimonides College
Secretary Maimonides College

The request for a new school made by the Congregation Rodef Shalom met with a general response, and at the annual meet-

' NOTE—At that time the numbers on houses were not arranged according to squares running north and south or east and west, but were numbered consecutively without reference to intervening streets.

ing of the Society, held May 23, 1852, in pursuance of the subject, the following formal communication from the Congregation Rodef Shalom was received:

PHILADELPHIA, May 21, 1852.

Gentlemen:

"Being fully impressed with the necessity of educating our children in our *own* schools where they can obtain an English as well as Hebrew education and having learned with the liveliest interest the progress of the scholars at the late examination of the schools under your direction; Last Monday night at a general meeting of the Congregation Rodef Shalom we were appointed a committee to form some feasible plan to have a school or schools to be supported by the different Congregations in this City for the instruction of our children under your superintendence.

LIEUT. JONATHAN M. EMANUEL
Secretary, 1857—1863

"We beg leave to state that the Congregation which we have the honor to represent have a school where the children of the members of the Congregation receive a German and Hebrew education, but as the children attend the public schools and afterwards ours, so that they have no time for recreation, it would therefore be preferable if they could attend a school where the Hebrew and English are taught together.

"Our school is supported from a tax on the seat holders and costs us $950; this amount our Congregation would willingly contribute if the other Congregations would in like proportion pay for the support of the schools.

"Should you think favorably of a plan to form a school or more on a larger scale and appoint a committee, we will call with them on the different Congregations and solicit their co-operation and support."

Yours Respectfully,

Signed { JACOB LANGSDORF,
{ JACOB MAYER.

MAYER FRANK
Board of Officers, 1856—1877

After a full discussion of the proposition thus formulated, the chair appointed I. Binswanger, I. Leeser and M. A. Dropsie to confer with the Committee of the Congregation and report at the next meeting of the Board of Managers, which report is as follows:

"The undersigned committee, appointed to confer with the committee of the Congregation Rodef Shalom on the proposition submitted by them to the Hebrew Education Society and any other committee that may apply for the same purpose, beg leave to report, that they have had a conference with Messrs. J. Langsdorf, J. Mayer and Sol. Keyser of the above named committee (none other having made application) and after an exchange of views and opinions came to the conclusion that the only feasible plan would be for the said Congregation to raise either by taxation, subscriptions and voluntary contributions, or by whichever means they may see proper, the necessary amount to meet the expenses which this Society would incur in opening another school for 160 pupils like the one already established, and then to enter into an agreement with the Board of the Hebrew Education Society for admitting the children of all

DAVID EGER
Charter Member

their members and seat-holders as full pay scholars, and under the established rules and regulations, by paying a certain amount per annum, and in order that the said Congregation may have its full share of the management of the schools, your committee suggested that all the members and seat-holders who are interested in the prosperity of the school might become members of the Society by paying $3.00 per annum (after being duly proposed and elected.)

"The probable expenses without reference to the furnishing of the school room were estimated by us at $1,800 per annum.

"Your committee learned with much pleasure that these propositions, as submitted to the Congregation Rodef Shalom by their committee, who made great exertions in their behalf, were warmly approved by the Congregation and the amount of $950 raised by them annually for educational purposes was at once appropriated, provided a sufficient amount can be raised to make up the difference of the sum necessary for the accomplishment of this project.

"A subscription list was started and the sum of $497 already subscribed, (the subscriptions to be paid quarterly and to be for three years.)

HYMAN POLANO
Teacher in Hebrew School
Prof. Maimonides College.   (Hebrew Literature)

"We trust that this undertaking may fully succeed and be as productive of good results to the Jewish youth of Philadelphia as the advancement of education and religious instruction always gives.

MASON HIRSH
Board of Officers, 1874—1876

"If the Congregation Rodef Shalom can and do offer the sum of $1,600 per annum for the tuition of their children, not exceeding 160 in number, and for every child above that number $10 additional per annum, your committee would respectfully recommend such offer to be accepted, provided the Hebrew Education Society has the use of their school room and its furniture for as long a period as the school remains in operation; we also hope that the accession of members will enhance the income of the Society one or two hundred dollars, while every one will then feel the importance of making up any deficiency that may arise.

The above is respectfully submitted

Signed { I. BINSWANGER,
I. LEESER,
M. A. DROPSIE,
Committee.

On motion of Mr. I. Leeser, seconded by A. T. Jones, the following was unanimously adopted:

"*Resolved*, That if the Congregation Rodef Shalom can secure to the Education Society the sum of $1,600 per annum for a number of scholars not exceeding 160, and $10 per annum for every additional one, that the School Directors be empowered to enter into the necessary arrangements to open an additional school, provided the said Congregation supply the school-room furniture."

LUCIEN MOSS
Board of Officers, 1874—1877
1884—1886

No further reference to this subject appears in the minutes of the Society, and the mattter seems eventually to have been left without further action. At this time, (1854-5) Solomon Solis was President of the Society, and Abraham S. Wolf the Chairman of the Board of School Directors. Although the membership-list was growing and many contributed liberally towards its support, the receipts were unequal to the expenditures. The Board of Directors recognized that something had to be done in order to meet the Society's obligations, and a plan to liquidate this indebtedness was proposed that was as unique as it was successful.

JOSEPH NEWHOUSE.
Charter Member
Board of Officers, 1848-1856

At a meeting of the Board of Managers, held October 26, 1854, a committee consisting of Moses Nathans, Hyman Polock, Isidore Binswanger, Z. A. Davis and Moses A. Dropsie, which had been appointed "to take into consideration the most feasible plan in order to raise funds for the benefit of the Society . . . ", made the following report:

"Your committee to take into consideration the most feasible plan to raise funds for the benefit of the Hebrew Education Society, beg leave to report that the following three propositions were submitted and considered by them:

1. To give a series of lectures on the subject of our 'Religion, History and Education' by the most eminent and available men.

2. To give a concert, provided the aid of Mr. Maretzek and his company can be secured.

3. To give a Ball, under the auspices of the Board of the Hebrew Education Society and thirteen gentlemen to be selected from the Jewish community in the City (in all 30) who are to appoint a committee of ten among themselves to serve as acting managers.

JULIUS STERN
Charter Member
Board of Officers, 1848-1856

The first proposition, your committee deems inexpedient at present, as the funds of the Society do not allow trying an experiment which leaves any doubt of its success.

The second was thought would prove most profitable to the Society, most welcome to the public and least troublesome to the Board, provided the gratuitous aid of Mr. Maretzek and at least part of his company, could be secured; the committee endeavored to meet Mr. M. to solicit his aid and hear his views on the subject, but failed in meeting him.

The third proposition would also, no doubt, promote the object of the Society, if the Board will it, and are ready to share the trouble a Ball imposes on them. All of which is respectfully submitted."

EDWIN W. ARNOLD
Secretary, 1861—1866

At a special meeting held November 28, 1852, the committee reported that it had been decided on to give a ball and names were suggested as managers; but at the meeting of December 12th, the secretary stated "that it was utterly impossible to get a sufficient number of gentlemen to serve as a Ball Committee, having personally notified most of those proposed, a majority of whom had declined." It was then resolved "to give a public dinner and invite to it several influential Israelites of Philadelphia, not members of the Society, as well as some men of national reputation, in order to give to the affair the necessary prominence and brilliancy." Abraham Hart was elected chairman or president of the " First Charity Dinner Committee ;" Joseph H. Cohen, L. J. Leberman, David Pesoa and Henry Cohen, vice - presidents ; Joseph Newhouse, treasurer, and Isidore Binswanger, secretary. The Fuel Society of Philadelphia, being without a regular income sufficient to defray its running expenses, was in the same predicament as the Hebrew Education Society, and it was decided that one-third of the proceeds of the dinner should be turned over to the Fuel Society. Lyon J. Levy, at that time the most prominent Jewish merchant in Philadelphia, was appointed chairman of the Committee of Arrangements with the Rev. Isaac Leeser, Abraham S. Wolf, M. Cauffman, Jacob Langsdorf, Mayer Arnold, Simon W. Arnold, Zadoc A. Davis, Hyman Polock, Abraham Finzi, Alfred T. Jones, Moses Nathans, Moses A. Dropsie, E. S. Mawson, B. Greenewald, Henry S. Allen, Samuel Elkin, M. D. Cohen, P. S. Rowland, S. Kayser, Lazarus Mayer, Joseph Einstein and Jacob Mayer. Abraham S. Wolf was chairman of the Dinner Committee, and the Committee on Collections were the following: L. J. Leberman, Isidore Binswanger, Joseph Newhouse, P. S. Rowland, Jacob Langsdorf, Abraham S. Wolf, M. Cauffman and Abraham Hart.

MAYER ARNOLD
Charter Member
Board of Officers, 1850—1860

JOSEPH SCHONEMAN
Charter Member
Board of Officers, 1848—1850

Two hundred and fifty dollars was subscribed by the Managers of the Society, to insure the success of the undertaking.

At a meeting of the Board of Managers held January 4, 1852, Mr. Hart, on behalf of the Committee for Collection, reported "that they have to the present time collected two hundred and twelve dollars, without having as yet called on any gentleman north of Market street..." The following resolution proposed by him (Mr. Hart) and seconded by Mr. Binswanger was unanimously adopted:

"*Resolved*, That the thanks of this meeting be tendered to the several gentlemen whose names are hereunto annexed for their generous and liberal donations in aid of the school established by the Hebrew Education Society, and that through their kindness the Managers hope to be enabled to continue the usefulness of the school, and that the Secretary be requested to send a copy of this resolution to the same."

Donors' names: A. Hart, D. L. Moss, M. Cauffman, J. L.

Dr. JACOB SOLIS COHEN
Board of Officers, 1864—1865
Secretary, 1867—1868

Moss, A. S. Wolf, H. Gratz, L. J. Levy, Mr. Lazarus, Mitchell & Allen, M. Nathans, S. Solis, G. Cromeline, A. Elkin, R. Cromeline, Jos. Newhouse, R. Mayers, I. Binswanger, H. Polock, L. Andrade.

At the Board meeting, February 15th, the following names were added: B. Lieber, D. Samuels, S. Nathan, W. Cromeline, H. Leveistein, Mindel & Bros., L. J. Phillips, H. Pincus, L. Berg, G. D. Rosengarten, L. Mayer, Lowengrund & Jacobs, P. Nathans, H. M. Phillips, Gans & Lieberman, D. Abrams, M. Moyer, Bloomingdale & Rhine, A. Oppenheimer, M. Arnold, Is. Hyneman.

AARON LAZARUS
Secretary, 1868–1870

At a meeting of the Board of Managers, held December 19, 1852, a letter from Mr. I. Binswanger, inclosing one from Mr. Jos. Seligman of New York, president of the H. B. S. of that city, was read as follows:

S. Solis, Esqr., President of the H. E. S., Philada.
Dear Sir:
The very lively interest I feel in the prosperity of our Society,

induced me when I found last Sunday "that sufficient encouragement was not given" to the projected Ball, to address a letter of inquiry to the President of the German H. B. S., of N. Y., in regard to a Dinner; hoping that since many of the gentlemen comprising our Board of Managers were so much more in favor of a Dinner than a Ball, one might perhaps be gotten up, yielding even a larger amount to our Society than a Ball would have done; I therefore take pleasure in enclosing to you herewith the answer received from N. Y.

You will please use your own discretion in calling a special meeting of the Board to consider the expediency of giving an Anniversary Dinner for the benefit of our Society and the Fuel Society or not.

SOLOMON THALHEIMER
Board of Officers, 1874—1876

Yours very Resp'y.
(Signed) I. BINSWANGER.

Dec. 16, '52.

[ENCLOSURE.—COPY.]

NEW YORK, 15 Decr., 1852.

Mr. I. BINSWANGER, Pha.

Dear Sir:

In reply to your inquiry respecting our Anniversary Dinner, I state to you the result of my experience at our last Dinner: The viands, without wine, with which we were furnished by Mr. Joseph Cohn, 56 Orchard St., viz. $1.25 per head, a Mr. A. Somers here furnishes, to my taste at least, a better dinner and charges $1.37½. We had about 325 guests; they drank some 25 baskets of Champagne and 10 doz. Hock, and smoked 2000 Segars; our room cost us $150. Music $30. The waiters were furnished by Cohn; our total expense was about $900. Our Rec'ts. $3,500. A very cheering result for our Society, and trust you may be equally successful in raising funds for your poor.

SIMON LIVERIGHT
Board of Officers, 1876—1877

With much Respect, Your friend and Serv.,
(Signed) JOS. SELIGMAN.

Owing to the absence of Mr. Binswanger at this meeting, the matter was deferred to an adjourned meeting held January 2, 1853, when " it was resolved that the Society should get up a dinner under the supervision of the Board and such other gentlemen as they may think fit to add to their number, for the benefit of this and the Fuel Society, ⅔ to the former and ⅓ to the latter, provided a Cosher dinner can be procured on satisfactory terms."

The " First Charity Dinner" was held on the evening of February 23, 1853, in the Sansom Street Hall (now occupied by MacKellar, Smiths & Jordan, typefounders, on Sansom street below Seventh). "Of the many

LEWIS M. ALLEN
Charter Member
Secretary, 1863

dinners that have been given in this city," said a writer (Arthur Cannon) in the *North American* of March 2, 1853, " which we have attended, this eclipsed them all in the order, propriety and good feeling manifested by the company, and the good taste that pervaded the whole of the arrangements, even the most minute, and which reflect great credit on the gentlemen who composed the Committee of Arrangements. Covers were laid for three hundred and fifty guests, and the dinner was prepared according to the Jewish custom in every particular. There was a bountiful supply of all the substantials, delicacies and luxuries of life; the wines and liquors were of the choicest kinds, and in great profusion. The confectionary, pastry and ornamental pieces were of a novel and beautiful description. The Hall was brilliantly illuminated by several massive chandeliers, in addition to which there were numerous wax candles, which diffused a soft and mellow light over the tables . . . At a quarter past seven o'clock Beck's celebrated band, with their new silver instruments, struck up a march when the President (Abraham Hart) entered the dining-hall, accompanied by two of the speakers, and followed by the members of the Committee of Arrangements, each accompanying someone of the distinguished guests."

MYER D. COHEN
Charter Member
Board of Officers, 1849—1852
1854—1855

The President was supported on his right by George M. Dallas, former Vice-President of the United States; Rev. Dr. Morris Raphall, of New York; William B. Reed, then District Attorney of Philadelphia and a well-known literary man; Morton McMichael, and others; and on the left by Dr. Morais; Charles Gilpin, then Mayor of Philadelphia;

JULIUS DAVIDSON
Charter Member

the Rev. Samuel M. Isaacs, of New York; the Rev. Isaac Leeser and David Paul Brown. The Rev. S. Morais opened the banquet with a prayer, and said grace after meat in Hebrew, when the goodly company had regaled themselves.

H. DuBOLE
Charter Member
Board of Officers, 1858—1865
1866—1868

George M. Dallas responded to the toast, "Civil and Religious Liberty," and his response was especially fine. In answering to the toast, "The Patriots of the Revolution," William B. Reed spoke of the part played by Jews in the war for independence. "There were Jewish soldiers in our ranks. There was Jewish blood shed on our soil. There are Jews now proud of their revolutionary lineage; and no word was said, no deed done by our Christian ancestors, whose wise counsels and brave spirits conducted and controlled the Revolution, to give pain or offence to that small but devoted and devout band, the followers of Israel, who being here, acted up to their steady principles of loyalty to the land where their lot is cast." Terse, eloquent and pregnant with wit were the responses of Morton McMichael, "The Press;" Isaac Leeser, "Education;" Moses A. Dropsie, "Our Glorious Mission;" Mayor Gilpin, "Philadelphia;" and the others, all of which, a chronicler relates, the audience received with "prolonged and enthusiastic applause."

AARON ISAACS
Charter Member

Over five thousand dollars was received by the managers of the First Annual Charity Dinner, of which two thousand five hundred dollars ($2,524.64) went into the coffers of the Hebrew Education Society. So successful in every way was this, the virgin effort of the Board of Managers, that it was resolved to make the banquet an annual affair and thus make permanent an enterprise, the only object of which was to fill the depleted treasuries of Philadelphia's Jewish charities.

The second dinner was held on Thursday evening, February 2, 1854, in the hall on Sansom street. Abraham Hart again served as President and Joseph Newhouse as Treasurer. The vice-presidents were L. J. Leberman, Isidore Binswanger, David Pesoa and Abraham S. Wolf. Abraham Finzi acted as secretary. Solomon Solis was chairman of the Committee on "Toasts," Simon W. Arnold on "Arrangements," Abraham S. Wolf on "Dinner," L. J. Leberman on "Collections."

JULIUS JACOBS
Charter Member

Morton McMichael, William B. Reed, Charles Gilpin, Dr. Isaacs and Dr. Raphall again graced the occasion with their presence. There were also present Dr. J. K. Mitchell, William Birney, the Rev. Jacob Frankel (who said grace in Hebrew) and Benjamin Harris Brewster, later Attorney General of the United States. Dr. Mitchell responded to the toast, "Our Sister Charities," and Mr. Brewster spoke with rare wit and eloquence upon "Civil and Religious Liberty." The last toast, "Consolidation,—the consolidation of the City and County of Philadelphia this week in our legislative halls; the consolidation of the friends of humanity of all creeds this evening in our dining hall," was drunk with great fervor and enthusiasm by all the gentlemen present. Moses A. Dropsie, who had been

ISRAEL JACOBS
Charter Member

HEBREW EDUCATION SOCIETY.

again asked to respond to one of the toasts, was absent by reason of the death of his mother. This dinner has been called one of the notable events in Philadelphia Jewish history.

The receipts from the second banquet gratified the managers and those interested in getting it up,—three thousand dollars was distributed among the societies. The Hebrew Education Society received two-thirds and the remainder was divided among the Hebrew Fuel Society, the Ladies' Hebrew Benevolent Society, the Ladies' German Benevolent Society, the Ladies' Hebrew Sewing Society and the United Hebrew Benificient Society. The year following a ball was given instead of a dinner and proved such a success financially that it was thought expedient to continue this form of entertainment, and thus the Hebrew Charity Ball Association sprang into existence. It owes its origin to the members of a committee appointed by the President of the Hebrew Education Society, and it is this small band of devoted workers that made possible the association that annually gives a ball with such good

ALFRED T. JONES
Board of Officers, 1848—1850
Secretary, 1850—1854
Board of Officers, 1854—1862
Vice-President, 1862—1867
Board of Officers, 1867—1870

results for the benefit of the Jewish poor of Philadelphia. There had been some changes in the faculty of the

REV. JACOB FRANKEL

school. Michael M. Allen and Miss Bomeisler had resigned, and it was necessary to fill their places. Jacob Mendez De Solla was elected principal, Mr. Edward H. Weil, instructor in the English branches; Miss Willelmina Todd, Miss Marion Monachesi and Miss E. J. Wright, assistant teachers. The rooms in the Phoenix Hose House were no longer large enough to accomodate the increasing number of pupils who attended the sessions, and it was resolved to secure more commodious quarters. The old Baptist church property on the east side of Seventh street, between Callowhill and Wood streets, was purchased and the building thoroughly renovated. It was dedicated on November 12, 1854, and the Rev. Isaac Leeser, Moses A. Dropsie, Dr. Morais, Rev. Gabriel Papé, Rev. Lazarus Naumberg and the Rev. Jacob Frankel took part in the services. The Hebrew Sunday School Society vacated their rooms in the Phoenix Hose House at this time, and the schools were established in the Education Society's new edifice on Seventh street.

The community of interest which the Hebrew Education Society centered through its activity at this period, is indicated by the following extract from the minutes of the meeting of the Board of Managers held August 3, 1856, when "a communication from the Congregation Rodef Shalom was received and

MICHAEL REINHARD
Charter Member

read, asking for the use of the lower room of the school house, Seventh and Wood streets) as a temporary synagogue.

It was resolved, "that the use of the lower room of the school house be granted to the Congregation Rodef Shalom free of charge, with the restriction that such use of the room is not to interfere with the permission given to the Hebrew Sunday School to occupy the same, and also that gas may be introduced at the expense of the Congregation."

The society suffered a great loss in June, 1854, in the death of its first President, Solomon Solis, who had uninterruptedly served since its foundation as its executive officer and as member of the Board of School Directors. Abraham S. Wolf was unanimously elected in his stead. The officers for the following year (1855) were: Abraham S. Wolf, president; Rev. Isaac Leeser, vice-president; Abraham Hart, treasurer; M. M. Allen, secretary, and A. Finzi, assistant secretary. The Board of Managers: M. A. Mitchell, Mayer Arnold, M. A. Dropsie, Hyman Polock, Isidore Binswanger, A. T. Jones, Jacob Mayer, L. J. Leberman, David Pesoa, Jos. Newhouse, M. Cauffman and Solomon Gans, Sr. Isidore Binswanger was chairman of the Board of School Directors. The names of over one hundred and seventy pupils were upon the

SAMUEL HECHT
Secretary, 1870—1871

rolls of the Society's schools, and the progress made by them was satisfactory in every way. The staff had been increased from three to seven members.

DAVID H. SOLIS
Charter Member
Board of Officers, 1848—1860
" " " 1863 1885

The first legacy bequeathed to the Hebrew Education Society has been the largest. Judah Touro, a public-spirited citizen of New Orleans, and well-known as a philanthropist, died on January 18, 1854, in the eightieth year of his age. To the Hebrew Education Society he bequeathed twenty thousand dollars.

The preparatory school continued to receive the active support of the public, and the educational advantages to be derived from attendance at its sessions, led to a large increase in the number of pupils. The attendance became more regular, and the reputation of the school increased. The president of the Hebrew Education Society, Abraham S. Wolf, in his annual report said, that "he had the pleasing intelligence to report that it (the school) had gained the reputation of being, if not superior, at least equal to any Hebrew school in the country."

In 1862 Abraham S. Wolf, after serving for eight years as presiding officer of the Education Society, declined a re-election. Desiring still to take an active interest in its work, he was elected a Director. Mr. Dropsie succeeded him as President.

LEOPOLD SULZBERGER
Charter Member

The following teachers have served in the day schools up to the present writing: Miss Evelyn Bomeisler,

Michael M. Allen, Miss Anna Murray, Miss Clara Weil, Jacob Mendez De Solla, Edward H. Weil, Miss Wilhelmina Todd, George F. Hitchcock, Miss Marion Monachesi, Miss E. J. Wright, Rev. L. Naumberg; Eugene Smyth, Miss Breen, Miss Julia Goodfellow, Rev. S. C. Noot, Michael Heilprin, (teacher in German, French and the classics, who resigned in 1858 to become assistant editor of the New American Cyclopedia; Miss Esther A. Davidson, Miss Julia B. Eckstein, John McClintock, Miss T. J. Donnelly, Mayer Sulzberger, Madame Marmillod, L. Buttenwieser, Hyman Polano, Miss Ellen Phillips, W. J. Flynn, W. J. Rogers, Miss Charity S. Cohen, William H. Williams, Aaron S. Bettelheim, Mr. Braunschweig, Miss Huckle, H. Max Gerstenkrantz, Solomon Solis-Cohen, M. E. Lam, Cyrus Adler, Henry Samuel Morais, Moses De Ford, George Seldes, Charles D. Spivak, Isaac Husik and Hyman Grabosky.

SIMON W. ARNOLD
Charter Member
Board of Officers, 1867—1861
" " 1868—1874
Trustee Maimonides College

BERNARD BLUM
Charter Member

Since the establishment of the Hebrew Education Society in 1848, the Jewish population had largely increased. Synagogues had sprung up all over the country. Many of them failed for lack of an efficient person to minister to the wants of the congregation. The incumbents were often men of scholarly attainments and well versed in Hebrew lore, but they could not speak English idiomatically and had not received the training so necessary for a theologian. The greater number of them were, by profession, Hebrew teachers,—and they were nothing more. The establishment of a theological seminary was as much a necessity in 1865, as the schools for the education of Jewish children had been sixteen years before.

No better illustration of the general conditions existing in the Jewish community of Philadelphia at this period can be afforded than by a citation of the Annual Report of the Society for 1864, which was apparently the first report printed for general circulation. We here append this document in full:

ANNUAL REPORTS

OF THE

HEBREW EDUCATION SOCIETY

OF

PHILADELPHIA.

Presented at the Meeting held on June 5th, 1864.

The Annual Meeting of this institution was held on Sunday, June 5th, at the school-house, when the following officers were elected to serve for the current year: Moses A. Dropsie, President; Alfred T. Jones, Vice-President; Abm. Hart, Treasurer; Edwin W. Arnold, Secretary; Abm. Finzi, Assistant Secretary; L. Binswanger, C. Bloomingdale, H. De Boer, Samuel Hecht, C. Johnson, Isaac Leeser, Augustus Mailert, Rev. Sabato Morais, Michael Moyer, D. H. Solis, S. Teller, and A. S. Wolf, Managers. The subjoined Reports were then presented, and it was resolved that they should be inserted in the *Occident*, and issued also in pamphlet form, in order to inform the public of the working of this Association. It will be seen from the Report of the chairman of the school committee, that it is contemplated to endeavor to enlist public sympathy with the work in hand, in order to collect the means to secure the establishment of a Hebrew College under the supervision of the Society, as its charter contemplates. It is needless for us to urge this matter on the attention of our friends, as we have done so often already. If the time for action has not yet come to commence a college for Israelites in this country, it must soon be so. Congregations not only increase by immigration, but also by the natural increase from children born in this country. But with the augmentation of numbers, knowledge has not progressed at an equal rate; wealth has abundantly multiplied under God's blessing, but the means of training our youth for the service of Heaven are still lamentably deficient. The question therefore resolves itself simply in this, Shall we make the effort, whether we fail or not, to erect a house for Jewish science in Philadelphia or elsewhere? The central position and general healthfulness of the climate, together with the easy access to good libraries, would point out Philadelphia as the future central seat for Jewish education; but we only express the general sentiment of our friends in stating, that no objection will be made on the part of our residents should the public good require the location of the school elsewhere. But let the effort only be made to start the good enterprise, and let all who have it at heart lay aside all sectional and local jealousy, and act as the best interests of religion demand. This is all we ask, and all that our Society contemplates by initiating the present movement.

REPORT OF THE CHAIRMAN OF THE BOARD OF SCHOOL DIRECTORS.

To the President and Members of the
Hebrew Education Society.

Gentlemen:

A number of years have elapsed since the custom of presenting an Annual Report to the Society has been discontinued; but as it is no doubt your wish to be informed of the progress of the Society and the school under its charge, I respectfully submit a statement of the affairs of the Society.

Through the exertions of the Managers, the investments of the Society have been kept almost unimpaired, a committee for the last three years having obtained voluntary contributions to cover the deficiency, which course, however, it is hoped will in future be obviated by every member securing at least an additional member, and by all uniting to promote the usefulness of the Society. The school is now in the fourteenth year of its existence, and is steadily, though quietly, progressing. The Rev. L. Buttenwieser, assisted by Mr. H. Polano, has charge of the Hebrew department, consisting of spelling, reading, grammar, translation, and a study of catechism. The English department is in the hands of Mr. John McClintock, assisted by Miss Esther Davidson and Miss Julia B. Eckstein, and comprises the following studies: spelling, reading, definition, grammar, etymology, geography, arithmetic, American history, English history, and natural philosophy. The German is taught by Mr. Buttenwieser and Latin by Mr. McClintock. The number of pupils on the roll at present is one hundred and eight (thirty-six girls and seventy-two boys), with the prospect of an increase after vacation, which will require the employment of an, other teacher for the primary class. Of the above number, sixty-six are non-paying pupils.

The expectation of the Managers that the number of pupils would increase to such an extent as to require branch schools, is not likely to be realized, as a number of congregational schools have been lately established, which naturally prevents that accession to our school which it would otherwise have received.—Viewing these congregational schools as auxiliaries to ours, it was deemed of the utmost importance, and consequently resolved, to form a theological class for boys not less than twelve years of age to be educated for the Jewish ministry, and that when sufficient support shall have been secured suitable professors be engaged to teach the higher branches. It has been our privilege, under the blessing of Providence, to call into existence an institution that has now stood the test of time, and may fairly challenge comparison with any educational establishment of the kind in the country.

Education, the greatest boon which we can leave our children, is here diffused to rich and poor alike. Children can receive religious instruction combined with all branches of an English education, and learn besides other languages without being obliged to go to several schools, or to have several private teachers for all the various branches, which gives children but little time for recreation. The founders of our Society have, with much forethought, obtained a charter to enable us to establish a High School or College. The late Judah Touro endowed our Society munificently; and shall we, the members of the Hebrew Education Society, longer permit this want in our city, nay, in our whole country, to exist, of having no institution, no house of learning, where our young men can be properly educated for the elevated position of teachers and ministers? At no time in the history of our beloved country have our people enjoyed a greater degree of material prosperity than at present. Congregations, springing up in all parts of the land, are anxious to engage capable men for their guides and instructors; but where is the college in the whole country that can offer the opportunity for our native young men to become there qualified for the position of expounding the law and giving instruction in the holy language?

No city is more centrally located for this purpose, nor is any Society better prepared to fill this want than ours. Let us therefore, collectively and individually, put forth our energies to carry out to the full extent the object of our Society, which is not controlled by any particular congregation, but recognizes only the cause of religious and scientific education in its broadest sense. Let us enlist every well-wishers of Israel here and elsewhere in the erection of a temple of learning worthy of the American Israelites; and, with God's blessing, we will leave to posterity the richest legacy we can give them. Let meetings of *all* the Israelites of the city be called at an early day, and let us see how large a permanent fund can be made up, or what ways and means can be devised to carry the above suggestion into execution.

Respectfully submitted,

(Signed) I. BINSWANGER,

Chairman Board of School Directors.

Philadelphia, June 3, 1864.

TREASURER'S REPORT.

HEBREW EDUCATION SOCIETY, IN ACCOUNT WITH A. HART, TREASURER, OF PHILADELPHIA.

1864.   DR.

June, To cash per orders Nos. 668 to 710 inclusive, as per vouchers herewith, to wit:

For salaries and teachers one year	$1,959 50	
For bills of books and stationery	243 72	
For cleaning rooms	135 00	
For bills of repairs to stoves, &c.	65 69	
For salary for Assistant Secretary one year	50 00	
For bills of coal 1863 and 1864	253 60	
For bills of sundries	20 49	
For int. on mortgage on school house one year	630 00	
For 5 per cent. commission for collecting $1,328.71 to collector	66 43	$3,424 43
" To cash paid for $1,000 7 per cent. Lombard and South St. 7 per cent. mortgage bond purchased per order of the Board		900 00
" cash paid for $12,500 U. S. 10-40 loan at 5 per cent. interest per order of committee of Board of Managers		12,500 00
		$16,824 43
June 5, To balance due A. Hart, Treasurer		$198 11

HEBREW EDUCATION SOCIETY. 51

1864.   CR.

June 5, By cash received interest on stocks, loans, and mortgage of the Society to date	$1,235 30
" " cash received for subscription of members and for tuition of children, per Mr. A. Finzi, collector	1,528 62
" " balance on hand May 17, 1863, as per account audited that date	19 40
" " donations received from the following gentlemen for 1863-64, to wit: (see below)	105 00
" " donations for 1862-63	10 00
" " cash received from congregation Mikve Israel (loan)	1,100 00
" " " " " mortgage paid in full	12,500 00
" " balance due Treasurer for this amount overpaid by him this day, as per account audited, with the vouchers, this date	198 11
	$16,824 13

E. & O. E.

(Signed)   A. HART, Treasurer.

Philadelphia, June 5, 1864.

Examined and audited with the vouchers, this 5th day of June, 1864, and also examined the certificates of stock and loans, and found them as follows:

  $ 3,700 city 6 per cent. Gas Loan.
    12,500 U. S. 5 per cent. 10-40 loan.
     2,000 7 per cent. 5th & 6th St. Frankford Passenger Railway.
     2,000 7 per cent. bonds Raritan and Delaware Bay Railroad.
     1,000 7 per cent. bonds Lombard and South Street Passenger Railway.
       400 in sixteen shares Mill Creek Railroad Company.

$21,600

           Signed,   ISAAC LEESER,
                               EDWIN W. ARNOLD.

LIST OF DONATIONS.

S. W. Arnold	$20 00	Wolf & Brother	5 00
I. Binswanger	20 00	Joseph L. Berg	5 00
C. Bloomingdale	20 00	Newberger & Hochstadter	5 00
M. A. Dropsie	20 00	H. Simpson	5 00
Solomon Gans	20 00	Edwin W. Arnold	5 00
A. Hart	20 00	Goldsmith & Brothers	5 00
Gans, Liberman & Co.	20 00	Hirsh & Brother	5 00
M. Moyer	20 00	A. Kahn	5 00
Teller, Anathan & Co.	20 00	S. Fernberger	5 00
A. S. Wolf	20 00	M. Seidenbach	5 00
M. Rosenbach	10 00	T. Mindel	5 00
Lewis Seidenbach	10 00	Hirsh & Gerstley	5 00
Leon Berg	10 00	M. Silberman	5 00
Henry Mayer	10 00	L. Walker	5 00
H. Guiterman	10 00	Hezekiah W. Arnold	5 00
Feustman & Kaufman	10 00	William B. Hackenburg	5 00
Blum, Rau & Co.	10 00	J. Cauffman & Son	4 00
Stern, Jonas & Co	10 00	A. Mailert	3 00
L. & S. Hecht	10 00	S. Vendig	3 00
Michael Jacobs	10 00	Stern & Brother	3 00
Isaac Rhine	5 00		
Potsdamer & Brother	5 00		$403 00

COLLECTED AFTER MAKING UP THE REPORT.

D. C. Levy	$15 00	Hyman Polock	5 00
Lazarus Mayer	10 00	Frank Brothers & Co	5 00
Joseph Newhouse	10 00	C. Johnson	5 00
H. De Boer	5 00	A. Kauffman	5 00
Nathan Hays	5 00	A. Straus	2 00
D. H. Solis	5 00		
Goldsmith & Liebman	5 00		$77 00

Rev. Dr. M. JASTROW
Vice President 1867-1874
Provost Maimonides College
(Talmud, Jewish Literature and Hebrew Philosophy)

On December 4, 1864, a meeting was held in the National Guard's Hall, Race street below Sixth, under the auspices of the Hebrew Education Society and the presidents of the various congregations in the city, for the purpose of considering the feasibility of establishing a Jewish Theological College. The call had been issued by a committee appointed by the President of the Education Society, and consisted of Isidore Binswanger, chairman, Moses A. Dropsie, Isaac Leeser, Charles Johnson and Samuel Hecht. Nothing of importance was done at this meeting. While this project was being agitated, it was resolved to apply to the State Legislature for a supplementary act to the Act incorporating the Society, so that the pupils of the schools of the Education Society could be admitted to the High Schools of the city without previous attendance in the public schools. Governor Curtin signed the act on April 11, 1866. By this the schools of the Hebrew Education Society took rank with the best grammar schools in

A. M. FRECHIE
Secretary, 1863—1864
Board of Officers, 1865—1866
" " 1876—1880
" " 1884—1885
Trustee Maimonides College

HENRY COHEN
Trustee Maimonides College

the city. This was a privilege possessed by no other private school in the First School District of Pennsylvania.

It was decided to establish the seminary under the joint auspices of the Hebrew Education Society and the Board of Delegates of American Israelites. Abraham Hart, Moses A. Dropsie, Isidore Binswanger, Charles Bloomingdale, A. E. Massman, Levi Mayer, Henry Cohen, Solomon Gans, Simon W. Arnold, A. M. Frechie and Mayer Sulzberger, of Philadelphia; Mayer S. Isaacs, A. S. Saroni and Henry Joseph, of New York; M. Umstadter of Norfolk, Va., and Moses Friedenwald of St. Louis, were the Trustees of the first Jewish theological college in the United States.

It was found necessary for the support of the college to create a permanent endowment fund, which afterwards became known as the "maintenance fund." It was upon this foundation that the college was established. Abraham Hart and Isidore Binswanger gave five hundred dollars each; L. J. Leberman, two hundred and fifty dollars; Moses

JACOB LANGSDORF
Charter Member
Board of Officers, 1848-1850
1852-1873

A. Dropsie, Morris Rosenbach, Lazarus Mayer, Charles Bloomingdale and Joseph Newhouse, two hundred dollars each; Rebecca Gratz, Bernard Abeles, Seligman Abeles and H. Marcus, one hundred dollars each. There were many other smaller subscriptions, and many agreed to give a certain amount annually. The college was formally opened on Monday, October 28, 1867.

HENRY SIMSON
Charter Member

Maimonides College was the name given to the institution. The course of study was very elaborate, for it was the intention of the Trustees to ground the pupils thoroughly in a knowledge of Jewish law and traditions. The Greek, Latin, German, French, Hebrew and Chaldaic languages (and their literatures), were in the curriculum; the natural sciences, history, mathematics, astronomy, moral and intellectual philosophy, constitutional history and the laws of the United States; belles lettres, homiletics, comparative theology; the Bible and its commentaries, the Mishna and its commentaries, the Talmud and its commentaries, Jewish history and literature, Jewish philosophy, Yad ha-chazakah, and Shulchan 'Aruch.

Isaac Leeser, who had long advocated the organization of a school of theology, became Provost of the Maimonides College and President of its Faculty. Abraham Hart was President and Mayer Sulzberger, Esq., Secretary of the Board of Trustees. The college was truly fortunate in the selection of its faculty, and it may be stated with due confidence, that no Jewish educational institution in this country had (or has now) upon its roll of instructors such dis-

LEON BERG
Charter Member

tinguished names as those of Leeser, Morais and Jastrow. Isaac Leeser held the chair of English literature, logic and homiletics ; Dr. Sabato Morais, Biblical exegesis ; Dr. Marcus Jastrow, the Talmud, Jewish literature and Hebrew philosophy ; Dr. Aaron S. Bettelheim, Mishna, Yad hachazakah and the Shulchan 'Aruch. (Dr. Bettelheim resigned in consequence of his appointment as Rabbi in Richmond); L. Buttenwieser, Hebrew and Chaldaic languages and literatures ; William H. Williams (secretary to the Faculty), Latin, mathematics and geography. At a later date Rev. George Jacobs became instructor in English literature and allied subjects, and Hyman Polano in Hebrew and Mishna. Provision was made by which students of Maimonides College were enabled to take certain courses in the University of Pennsylvania, for which the Univerity, with great generosity, charged but a nominal fee.

MAYER STERNBERGER
Charter Member

On May 9, 1869, Moses A. Dropsie, President of the Hebrew Education Society and of the Maimonides College, in his report to the Society, stated as follows :

"Twenty years have elapsed since the formation of this Society, and during that period great difficulties have beset it ; but the large number that have been educated at your school, and the character of your instruction, attest that your faithfulness and perseverance have overcome the threatened dangers. You were early convinced of the necessity of a higher mental training than that imparted in the school, where instruction was given only in the primary branches of an English and Hebrew education ; and you felt that, in this republic, where man's powers of

SIMON STERNBERGER
Charter Member

mental development are unrestrained by political or social causes, where rapid strides are made in the world's progress, where institutions for the acquisition of knowledge are rapidly multiplying; there should be established an institution of Jewish learning combined with all the knowledge that the higher educational institutions afford.

"At the original formation of your Society, provision was made for the establishment of a college, when the proper means were procured.

AARON LICHTEN
Secretary, 1874–1876
Board of Officers, 1876–1889

"After patiently waiting for years, the auspicious moment arrived and Maimonides College was founded.

"A year has passed since its formation; and I now propose to give some account of it. Primarily, it owes its existence to the Rev. Isaac Leeser, and none know better than you, his co-laborers in Jewish education, that for the advancement of Judaism he dedicated his existence. The establishment of this college was one of the cherished objects of his life; and at length, when his incessant efforts were rewarded by its formation, death closed his labors ere he saw the fruition of his hopes. His death is an irreparable loss to the College. In honor of his memory, the Trustees have termed the first professorship of the Talmud, the Leeser Professorship.

"The Trustees in the administration of the College have experienced the difficulties which have beset many of the American colleges. They have not received the support and encouragement which the enterprise merits. Nearly all the means that have been contributed have been furnished by the Jews of Philadelphia. To place the College on a permanent foundation whereby it may successfully accomplish its purpose, it is necessary that there be thoroughly organized efforts for its support. To this end appeals should be made to all who feel an interest in its success. Money is required not only to defray expenses necessarily incident to the College, but also for the payment of the board and lodging of those students who are unable to do so.

"Mr. Leeser bequeathed to the College his valuable library, a number of generous donors have presented valuable books and the Trustees have purchased a few at the recent sales at Amsterdam. I presume that these now form the best collection in the United States of works by Jewish authors on the Bible, Jewish Religion, Philosophy, Science, Oriental Philology, Literature, etc.

ABRAHAM ADLER
Vice President, 1874–1878
President, 1878–till death in 1880

"Renewed efforts should be made for its increase; many could contribute works of value that remain hidden or unused which if given to the Library would be productive of good. A building should be purchased for the exclusive use of the College, and therein proper provision could be made for an increased number of students. In this building the Library should be placed and properly supervised, and its exhibition might thus, by a kind of object teaching, demonstrate the necessity for its enlargement.

"I have thus endeavored to state briefly an account of Maimonides College. The early history of many of the American institutions of learning is a history of struggles, continued battles with adversity, till at length friends appeared and rescued them from peril.

SIMON MUHR
Treasurer, 1875—1876
Board of Officers, 1876—1877

"Within a recent period noble hearted men have endowed American colleges with munificent gifts, and have thus embalmed their names in honor to be remembered by remote ages. How long shall Maimonides College struggle? surely our people, by the recollection of the learning and devotion of our ancestors, have sufficient incentive without these examples to make this College a blessing and an ornament to American Judaism."

That both College and School were organized on a broad and comprehensive plan, larger indeed than the circumstances warranted, is perhaps sufficiently manifest from what has been noted above, but a further light is thrown upon this

A. E. MASSMAN
Trustee Maimonides College

aspect of the subject by the following extracts: In his Annual Report, May 20, 1855, the President stated:

"In conclusion let me say, that however difficult our task has been, the reflection that the school will eventually prove to be the most desirable institution for the education of Jewish youth in the United States, is sufficient compensation for all our labors, and therefore sincerely recommend to continue to persevere in their good work."

On June 5, 1859, the President said in his Annual Report:

"Although the school has not increased in numbers, I have yet the pleasing intelligence to report, that it has gained the reputation of being if not superior, at least equal to any other Hebrew School in the country."

It was on February 1, 1868, that Isaac Leeser died. He had come to Philadelphia in 1829, when he succeeded the Rev. Abraham Israel Keys as minister of the Congregation Mickvé Israel, and from that time to the close of his life he labored for the holy cause of education with a stout heart and ever-ready

MOSES FRIEDENWALD
Trustee Maimonides College

pen. He had scarcely exercised the duties of his office as Provost of Maimonides College when death called him away. Desiring that the society which he had founded should receive some profit from his work long after he had ceased to live, he bequeathed to the Hebrew Education Society the valuable library which he had gathered together with so much labor and patience. It contains his *handapparat*, or the books and pamphlets he had used in the immediate preparation of his notable work. It is rich in Rabbinic and Biblical literature and in the more modern controversial writings.*

Dr. CYRUS ADLER
Teacher in Hebrew School
Librarian, 1881—1894

* The value of this library as a storehouse of Jewish literature is attested by the extensive use made of it by various investigators of Jewish history and notably by the list of books taken out of the Leeser Library for the purposes of the Jewish Historical Society, reported at the annual meeting of the Hebrew Education Society in 1895, and which we here note in full, as follows:

1. Brackenridge, H. M.—Speeches on the Jew Bill.
2. Carillon, Rev. B. C.—Sermon delivered at the Spanish and Portuguese Synagogue in aid of the Beth Limmud Society.
3. Cohen, Solomon Jacob—Elements of the Jewish Faith.

The Leeser Library was catalogued by Dr. Cyrus Adler in 1883, when he was librarian to the Education Society. As

4. Cresson, Warder—The Good Olive Tree of Israel.
5. Jerusalem.
6. The Great Restoration and Consolidation of Israel in Palestine.
7. De la Motta, Jacob, M. D.—Discourses.
8. De Sola, Abraham—The Sanitary Institutions of the Hebrews.
9. Biography of David Aaron De Sola.
10. Valedictory Address.
11. Ish Tsadik.
12. Dropsie, Moses A.—Discourse delivered at the Synagogue Rodeph Shalom.
13. Dropsie, Moses A.—Panegyric on Isaac Leeser.
14. Jacobs, Rev. Solomon—A Theological Refutation of "An Affectionate Address to the Jews of Jamaica."
15. Dedication of New Synagogue Beth-El-Emeth.
16. Jacobs, William—The Jew's Reasons for Believing in One God only.
17. Hymns written for the use of Hebrew Congregations.
18. Loeb, Dr. Henri—The Road to Faith.
19. Menasseh Ben Israel—De Resurrectione Mortuorum.
20. Mickvé Israel—Hoc est Spes Israelis.
21. Nathan, Rev. M. N.—A Sermon.
22. A defense of the Ancient Rabbinical Interpretation of Deut. XXIII, 3.
23. Newman, Selig—The Challenge Accepted.
24. Remarks of John McMahon in the House of Delegates of Maryland.
25. Persecution of Jews in the East, containing the proceedings of a meeting held at the synagogue Mickvé Israel.
26. Peixotto, Daniel L. M., M. D.—A Discourse.
27. The Jew; being a Defence of Judaism.
28. Bikkuré Hajam—The First Fruits of the West.
29. The Jewish Chronicle, edited by John Lillie.
30. Sinai, Ein Organ für Erkentness und Veredlung des Judenthums.
31. Moreh—The Guide, edited by Raphael D. C. Lewin.
32. Der Israelitsche Volksfreund, edited by C. M. Cohen.
33. Raphall, M. J.—Judaism Defended against the Attacks of T. J. C., of Oxford.
34. The Constancy of Israel.
35. The Path of Immortality.
36. The Bible View of Slavery. (Raphall.)
37. Salomon, Dr. G.—Twelve Sermons delivered in Hamburg.
38. Salomon, Rev. Dr. Louis—The Mosaic System.
39. Seixas, J.—A Manual of Hebrew Grammar.
40. Yisachar ben Yitschack—Jerusalem, oder Ueber den Zweck der Mosaischen Gesetzgebung.

*Catalogue of the Leeser Library, compiled by Cyrus Adler, A. B., Philadelphia, 1883; 12 mo., pp. 165.

a tribute of respect to the memory of Isaac Leeser, the first professorship of the Talmud in Maimonides College was called

ISAAC HYNEMAN
Board of Officers, 1870—1873

the "Leeser Professorship." A panegyric on his life and character was pronounced by Moses A. Dropsie, Esq., before the Hebrew Education Society on February 19, 1868.* Dr. Marcus Jastrow succeeded Isaac Leeser as Provost of the college.

As a desirable addition to the history of this noble-hearted enterprise and as recording the thoroughness with which it was planned and organized, we here subjoin a full citation of the rules and regulations for the government of Maimonides College:

The Faculty of Arts is composed of the following Professorships:
A Professorship of Homiletics, Belles Lettres and Comparative Theology.
A Professorship of the Bible and Biblical Literature.
A Professorship of Talmud, Hebrew Philosophy, Jewish History and Literature.
A Professorship of Mishnah with Commentaries, Shuchan Aruch and Yad ha-Chazakah.
A Professorship of Hebrew and Chaldaic Languages.
A Professorship of Greek and Latin Languages.
A Professorship of Rhetoric and English Literature.
A Professorship of Mathematics.
A Professorship of Natural Philosophy and Chemistry.

MARTIN SEIDENBACH
Charter Member

Panegyric on the Life, Character and Services of the Rev. Isaac Leeser, pronounced by Moses A. Dropsie before the Hebrew Education Society of Philadelphia, on February 19, 1868, (5628), 12 mo., Philadelphia, 1868.

A Professorship of German and French Languages.

OF THE FACULTY.

1. The Professors shall constitute "The Faculty of Arts," to whom, as a body, shall be committed the immediate regulation and government of the Collegiate Department, subject to the rules and statutes and the control of the Board of Trustees.

2. The College shall be under the supervision of the Provost, who shall make report in relation to it to the Board at least once a year.

3. Stated meetings of the Faculty shall be held every month, for the purpose of administering the general discipline of the College; and special meetings, as often as the business of the institution may require, to be called by the Provost or a majority of the members. At all meetings of the Faculty, the Provost shall preside, or in his absence a chairman can be elected.

4. The Faculty shall appoint a Secretary from its own body whose duty it shall be to keep the minutes of their proceedings, which shall be, at all times, open to the inspection of the Trustees.

5. No proceedings of the Faculty shall be considered as valid,

ISAAC BOSSKAM
Board of Officers, 1876–1878   Board of Officers, 1880–1894
Vice President, 1878–1880   Vice President, 1894–1895
President, 1880–1881   President, 1895–1898
Late Member of Board.

unless passed by a majority of the members at a meeting formally constituted.

6. It shall be the duty of the **Faculty** to make reports to the Board at their stated meetings, upon the state of the Collegiate department, stating particularly the names and residences of such students as have been admitted into, or have left the institution since the last report, with such remarks as they may deem expedient.

7. It shall be the special duty of the Provost, to visit and superintend the various departments; to see that the rules and statutes are duly carried into effect, to report to the Board every instance of refusal and neglect to comply with such rules and statutes, and to advise and suggest such alterations and improvements as he may deem best calculated to promote the welfare and usefulness of the institution.

SIMON B. FLEISHEL.
Treasurer, 1876—1883;
Board of Officers, 1883—1888.

OF THE CLASSES.

1. The students shall be distributed into five classes.

2. No applicant shall be admitted into the Freshman class under the age of 14; any special exception shall be decided by the Board.

upon the application of the Faculty. His fitness must appear on examination, to be conducted by the Professors, who must concur in opinion that he is qualified in such branches as shall be prescribed by the Board.

The requisites for entering the Freshman class shall be as follows:

LATIN—Cæsar, Virgil, Sallust, Odes of Horace.

ENGLISH—The elements of English grammar and of modern Geography.

HEBREW—The translation of the historical portions of the Bible with facility.

ARITHMETIC, including fractions and extraction of roots.

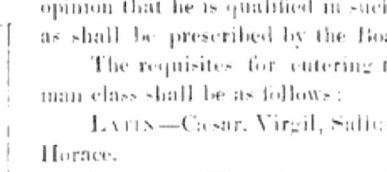

MORRIS KOHN
Board of Officers, 1876-1877

4. The Faculty shall keep a book called the Matriculation book, in which every candidate for entrance into this College shall, on his admission, have his name, age and residence entered, and the name and residence of his parent or guardian.

5. No student shall be admitted to advanced standing, without being as fully instructed as the class to which admission is asked, in all the studies in which the class has been instructed.

6. Vacation shall be from the 10th of July to the 31st of August.

COURSE OF INSTRUCTION.

1. The subjects of instruction in the institution shall be the following:—

Greek, Latin, German, French, Hebrew, Chaldaic and their literatures, the Natural Sciences, History, Mathematics, and Astronomy, Moral and Intellectual Philosophy, Constitutional History and Laws of the United States, Belles Lettres, Homiletics, Comparative Theology, the Bible with its commentaries, the Mishnah with its commentaries, the Shulchan 'Aruch, Yad ha-chazakah, Jewish History and Literature, Hebrew Philosophy and the Talmud with its commentaries.

DAVID SOLIS COHEN
Board of Officers, 1877-1878

2. At the close of each yearly term there shall be held an examination of all the classes in the presence of a Committee of the Board, and of such other Trustees as shall attend; after every examination the students who are distinguished in each class shall be arranged in the order of merit.

3. No student shall be suffered to proceed to a higher class who shall not, on examination, show himself master of the studies of the preceding year, but he may be allowed the privilege, (if the faculty shall judge it expedient to grant it,) of a second examination for admission thereto, at the opening of the next succeeding year.

4. Punishment shall be exclusively directed to a sense of duty, and the principles of honor and shame, and shall consist of private admonition by a Professor—admonition in the presence of the Faculty—admonition in the presence of the Faculty and of the class of the offender—removal to a lower class—suspension for a limited time from college—dismissal—expulsion.

5. No punishment except private admonition shall be inflicted, unless ordered by a resolution of a majority of the whole of the Faculty; nor shall the punishment of expulsion be inflicted unless it be first sanctioned by a vote of the Trustees. In case of dismissal, the offender may be re-admitted, but the effect of expulsion shall be an utter disqualification of the individual for re-admission into this institution, or of receiving any of its honors.

6. The fees for tuition of each year shall be one hundred dollars, payable at the commencement thereof; and no student shall be considered as entitled to his seat in the class for the term, until such payment is made. Notice that the tuition money is due, and that the Treasurer will at times attend (the time then to be stated) shall be given by the Secretary.

EDWIN ARNOLD
Board of Officers, 1876–1877

JACOB MILLER
Board of Officers, 1877–1878

7. The Board sanction the institution of a Literary Society, to consist of the students and alumni of the college, or such of them as shall be admitted members thereof, when suitable rooms can be appropriated for their use. The said society to be under the general control and supervision of the Faculty.

OF COMMENCEMENTS AND CONFERRING DEGREES IN THE ARTS.

1. There shall be an annual commencement of graduates in the arts on the last Thursday morning of each term, at 10 o'clock.

2. Candidates for the degree of Bachelor in the Arts or Divinity shall be publically examined by the Faculty in the collegiate departments, in the presence of the Committee of Examination and such other members of the Board of Trustees as may attend.

3. The Provost shall report the names of those

DAVID SULZBERGER.
Secretary, 185—

who shall have been found worthy of receiving such degree to the Board who shall, if the report be approved, confer such degree accordingly. But no degree shall be conferred unless by the vote of the Trustees; and every student, before he can be recommended for the degree of Bachelor of Arts or Divinity, shall settle his account with the Treasurer.

4. The Degree of Master of Arts may be conferred on the Alumni of the College, who shall have been Bachelor in the Arts of three years standing, and shall apply for that honor.

5. The order of the commencement shall be directed by the Faculty.

At no time during the history of the college did a great number of students matriculate, and few graduated and received their degrees. Among those who were trained for the Jewish ministry were Mr. Marcus Eliezer Lam, now a teacher in the Hebrew School of the Education Society at Touro Hall; Rev. David Levy, now of New Haven, Conn., and the Rev. Dr. Samuel Mendelsohn, at present minister of the Jewish synagogue of Wilmington, N. C.

CHARLES J. COHEN
Board of Officers, 1877–1880

Year after year the reports of the President and Treasurer gave evidence that the public never thoroughly favored or appreciated the work of the Society, and that its management was not conducted on a business basis. The fund which had been left to the Society by Judah Touro was constantly decreasing, yet we notice that teachers were continually asking for additional pay, and in most instances the increase was granted.

At a meeting of the Board held June 21, 1868, on motion of Mr. Abraham S. Wolf it was carried, "that the Board send a letter to Mrs. A. Hart, Mrs. Levi Mayer, Mrs. G. Silberberg, Mrs. L. Binswanger and Mrs. A. E. Massman, requesting them to take the initiatory

JACOB LOEB
Board of Officers, 1877–1882

steps towards calling a meeting of ladies, for the purpose of holding a Fair for the benefit of the Hebrew Education Society; and on motion of Dr. Jastrow that the communication be placed in the hands of a committee of three to call upon the ladies mentioned, was also agreed to." Drs. Jastrow and Bettelheim and Mr. Heilbron were appointed the committee.

Mrs. Abraham Hart declined to serve, and Mrs. Henry Cohen's name was substituted.

At a subsequent meeting a motion of Dr. Jastrow was adopted "that a committee be appointed to confer with the Board of Directors of the Jewish Hospital relative to coming to some definite understanding about the proposed 'Fair,' and that they have full power to act."

ISAAC SALLER
Board of Officers, 1877—1881
Vice-President, 1881—1886
Board of Officers, 1886—1892

The President appointed on the committee Messrs. A. Hart, L. Binswanger and Jos. Heilbron.

At the next meeting of the Board of Managers, "Mr. A. Hart made a verbal report on Fair, stating that the committee from the Hebrew Education Society had met a similar committee from the Jewish Hospital Association and the latter declined to act in conjunction with us as they deemed it inexpedient at the present time, they having other methods of raising money."

The holding of the "Fair" was therefore abandoned.

At the Board meeting of December 18, 1870, the following offered by Mr. M. Sulzberger was adopted: "Resolved—that some proper person be requested by the President to deliver a paid lecture at some time that may be agreeable to him, before the Israelites of Philadelphia, on the subject of Hebrew Education."

HENRY FRIEDBERGER
Board of Officers, 1878-1880

At the meeting held March 19, 1871, the President reported that in accordance with the resolution of the Board, adopted at its last meeting, he had requested the Rev. Dr. Jastrow to deliver a lecture upon the subject of Hebrew education, in aid of this Society, but that gentleman having refused, he (the President) then conferred with Mr. S. Wolf, of Washington, making a similar request of him, to which he at once consented, but a previous engagement to give an unpaid lecture in the German Synagogue prevented an arrangement satisfactory to all.

At a special meeting of the Board of Managers, held October 6, 1872, the Treasurer made a verbal report showing a very melancholy state of the finances of the Society, and expressing the belief that under the present circumstances the school could not continue to exist much longer.

HENRY C. DALSEMER
Board of Officers, 1880-1882

The following resolution offered by Mr. Mayer Sulzberger was adopted and referred to the Committee on the reestablishment of the School: "Resolved—That a committee of —— be appointed to confer with the Congregations Mickvé Israel and Beth-El Emeth, with a view to transfer to the said Congregations the building and furniture of this Society, under an express agreement and condition that certain arrangements for teaching the Hebrew language and its literature shall be forever kept up in such manner and under such restrictions as may be determined on."

Various resolutions in this direction were adopted at most of the meetings of the Society and Board, but no definite action was taken until December, 1873, when the work of Maimonides College was discontinued, after an activity extending through six years. The organization as such remained in existence, and at the annual meeting, held May 17, 1874, the Trustees elected were: B. J. Hart, A. M. Freehie,

LOUIS GERSTLEY
Assistant Secretary, 1877
Board of Officers, 1878–1884

Solomon Gans, Simon W. Arnold, Mayer S. Isaacs, A. S. Solomons, Myer Stein.

The expenses necessary to maintain the college were paid by the generous contributions of citizens of Philadelphia, in spite of the fact that it was a national institution open to the reception of students from all parts of the country. The contributions of money, which citizens of New York seemed so eager to subscribe to the college when its objects were first set forth, were not forthcoming. Lack of financial aid from other cities and a want of interest in the undertaking, led to its discontinuance. The Jewish Theological Seminary in New York is in a measure the successor of Maimonides College. It was instituted in 1886, chiefly through the efforts of Dr. Morais.

MICHAEL M. ALLEN
Board, 1853—1854
Secretary, 1854—1857
Board of Officers, 1858—1863
1865—1896
First Hebrew Teacher

The growth of the educational movement, which has become so marked within recent years and which has manifested itself especially in the domain of Jewish history and literature, may very justly be regarded as indicating the possibility of re-establishing Maimonides College on the lines planned for it by its projectors, and on a basis that would afford the institution that security and permanence which earlier conditions appear to have precluded. In such event the valuable franchise which the Hebrew Education Society possesses in its charter could be adequately utilized, and the educational system of the Society be thereby made complete. Thus the labors of Isaac Leeser, the self-devotion of Sabato Morais, the philanthropy of Judah Touro would be brought to fruition, and the hopes and aspirations of their earnest-hearted coadjutors be ultimately realized.

MOYER FLEISHER
Board of Officers, 1888—1892
President, 1892—1895

The twenty-fifth anniversary of the Hebrew Education Society was celebrated on Saturday evening, April 1, 1876, at Concordia Hall, on Callowhill street below Fifth street. Rev.

S. Morais opened the ceremony with a prayer, and Moses A. Dropsie, Esq., Dr. Marcus Jastrow and the Rev. George Jacobs

L. J. LEBERMAN
Board of Officers, 1852–1856

delivered addresses. The main portion of the programme consisted of songs and recitations by the children then attending the schools of the Society.

In the Fall of 1876, the Congregation Rodef Shalom was accorded the use of the Education Society's school house on 7th street near Wood, for the requirements of its congregational school, which was there continued until removed in 1879 to the school house of the Congregation on North 8th street.

The Society has been drawn into competition with two great educational systems, namely, as to the English branches, the public schools; and in Hebrew studies, with the congregational schools, and it proceeded at once to meet these altered conditions. A Hebrew school was opened on March 3, 1878, in the committee-room of the Congregation Bené Israel (Children of Israel), on Fifth street above Catherine street. A third school (the teaching of Hebrew still continued in the school house on Seventh street) was opened on October 12, 1879, at the northwest corner of Marshall street and Girard avenue. At this time Isidore Binswanger was President of the Hebrew Education Society, having succeeded Moses A. Dropsie in 1870, who had declined

DAVID PESOA
Board of Officers, 1850–1852
1853–1860

a re-election after having served continuously for eight years. In 1878, Isidore Binswanger, who had been a most active

SAMUEL STERNBERGER
Board of Officers, 1880-1887

worker for over twenty-seven years, also declined a re-election. Both he and Mr. Dropsie, by virtue of their office of President of the Hebrew Education Society, served as President of Maimonides College.

In 1878, Abraham Adler, a staunch supporter of the Society for many years, was elected to the presidency, but he died on November 9, 1879, during his term of office. Mr. Isaac Rosskam, who had been a manager of the Society for over two years, and its Vice-President at that time became president. In 1876 Abraham Hart, who had served as treasurer for twenty-seven years, ever since the Society was organized, resigned. His term of uninterrupted service in any one office, has been longest in the annals of the Society.

At the annual meeting, held March 14, 1880, D. Sulzberger, Simon A. Stern and Charles J. Cohen were appointed a committee to revise the By-Laws. This committee reported at the annual meeting, March 13, 1881,

ABRAHAM FINZI
Assistant Secretary, 1848-1868

78   HEBREW EDUCATION SOCIETY.

and the following was adopted with the exceptions noted:

OF MEMBERS.

Section 1. Any Israelite, aged at least twenty-one years, may become a Member of the Society upon the payment of the annual dues prescribed in these By-Laws for Members, Patrons and Friends.

Sec. 2. The annual dues of Members shall be five dollars; Patrons, twenty-five dollars, and Friends, one hundred dollars.

* *Sec. 3.* Any Member paying into the funds of the Association two hundred and fifty dollars, shall be declared a Life Member, and be subject to no further dues.

Sec. 4. A Member one year or more in arrears shall neither vote nor hold office, unless exonerated from his dues by the Board of Managers.

* Additions subsequently made.

LEVI MAYER.
Board of Officers, 1874—1883
Treasurer, 1883—1891
Trustee Maimonides College

Sec. 5. A Member more than two years in arrears may be dropped from the roll by a vote of the Board.

"*Sec. 6.* No person shall become a Member, nor exercise any of the privileges of membership who shall not have paid one year's dues, and not until after the adjournment of the meeting at which the applicant for membership shall have been proposed therefor.

OF OFFICERS.

Section 1. The officers of this Society shall be a President, Vice-President, Treasurer, Secretary and fifteen Managers, four of whom may be females, who, together, shall constitute the Board of Officers, and who shall also be Trustees of the College. At the first election, one-third of the Managers shall be chosen for one year, one-third for two years, and the remaining third three years, and at every subsequent election they shall be chosen for three years. "* Any one who shall have served for ten or more years as President, Vice-President, Treasurer or Honorary Secretary, or shall have served as a member of the Board of Officers for a period of not less than fifteen years, may be elected by the Society at its annual meeting, as an Honorary Member of the Board of Officers, for life, and be entitled to all the rights and privileges of any other member of the Board."

JACOB SULZBERGER
Board of Officers, 1881—1884

JACOB MUHR
Board of Officers, 1881—

The President, Vice-President, Treasurer and Secretary shall hold their respective offices for

* Additions subsequently made.

one year, or until their successors shall have been chosen.

Sec. 2. Elections shall be held at the annual meetings of the Society.

Sec. 3. The President shall preside at all meetings of the Society and Board of Officers, and shall draw orders on the Treasurer for the amounts passed by the Board of Officers; shall, whenever he may deem it necessary, convene special meetings of the Society or Board of Officers, and shall appoint all committees, unless otherwise ordered by the Society. He shall have the right to draw an order on the Treasurer for any sum not exceeding twenty-five dollars, without an appropriation by the Board. He shall be custodian of the seal of the Society, and shall, at the expiration of his term of office, deliver to his successor the said seal and all other property of the Society that may be in his possession.

HENRY MITCHELL.
Board of Officers, 1880-1884

Sec. 4. The Vice-President shall, in the absence of the President succeed to all his rights and duties.

Sec. 5. The Treasurer shall take charge of all moneys and securities of the Society, shall pay all orders duly signed by the President, or acting President, shall keep an account of his receipts and disbursements, and furnish a statement of the same at the annual meeting of the Society, and shall report at every stated meeting of the Board the amount of the balance in his hands. He shall give such security for the faithful performance of his duties as shall be approved of by the Board, and within two weeks after the election of

MARK SCHWARTZ
Board of Officers, 1886-1889

his successor, he shall deliver to the latter all moneys, papers, accounts and all other property whatsoever belonging to the Society.

Sec. 6. The Secretary shall keep fair and correct minutes of all transactions of the Society or Board of Officers, countersign all orders drawn by the President, shall prepare notices for all meetings, shall keep the accounts with the members of the Society, shall prepare all bills, and shall perform all duties incident to the office; for which service he shall receive such compensation as may be fixed by the Board of Officers.

WILLIAM GERSTLEY
Board of Officers, 1881—1885
1895—1898

Sec. 7. The Board of Officers shall fill all vacancies occurring among their own number, shall elect the School Teachers, shall employ an Assistant Secretary, Librarian, Messenger and Collector, and compensate them, shall determine the branches of education to be taught in the Schools, and shall do all things necessary for their government and maintenance.

Sec. 8. The seat of any member of the Board of Officers who shall absent himself from three consecutive stated meetings, without satisfactory excuse, may be declared vacant.

Sec. 9. All elections for officers or members of the Society shall be by ballot.

OF MEETINGS.

Section 1. The annual meeting of the Society shall be held on the second Sunday in March.

The fiscal year shall begin on the first of March.

LEVI GOLDSMITH
Board of Officers, 1879—1882

Sec. 2. The Board of Officers shall meet on the second Sunday in each month.

Sec. 3. Special meetings of the Society or Board of Officers may be called by the President whenever he may deem it necessary, and it shall be his duty to call such special meetings of the Society when requested by ten members thereof, and of the Board of Officers when requested by three of its members.

Sec. 4. At the meetings of the Society, fifteen shall constitute a quorum; of the Board, five.

JACOB WOLF
Board of Officers, 1881

OF THE SCHOOL DEPARTMENT.

Section 1. In the schools there shall be imparted religious instruction, Biblical History and the Hebrew language.

Sec. 2. The Board of Officers shall make all regulations governing the admission of pupils to the Schools, and also all rules in regard to the governing and management of the Schools.

Sec. 3. No pupil shall be admitted into the School without a written order from one of the members of the Board of Officers.

LEGACIES AND INVESTMENTS.

Section 1. All legacies to the Society shall be invested, and called by the name of the legatee. All funds received as legacies, or from life memberships, to remain intact forever, the interest only to be applied for educational purposes.

LOUIS E. LEVY
Board of Officers, 1882—

Sec. 2. No money of the Society shall be invested in any other than City of Philadelphia, State of Pennsylvania, or

United States securities, or first mortgages on property in the city of Philadelphia not owned by the Society.

RULES OF ORDER

Section 1. At all meetings the order of business shall be as follows:

(1) Roll-call.

(2) Reading of the minutes of the previous meeting.

(3) Reports of Officers.

(4) Communications.

(5) Election of Officers or Members.

(6) Deferred business.

(7) New business.

Sec. 2. The yeas and nays shall be entered on the minutes when requested by two members.

EDWARD L. ROTHSCHILD
Board of Officers, 1884–1889

OF AMENDMENTS

Section 1. No alteration, amendment or addition to these By-Laws shall be made, unless proposed at one meeting of the Society or Board of Officers, and confirmed at the next meeting of the Society by a vote of two-thirds of the members present, the Secretary having sent proper notice of such amendment to all the members: *Provided, however,* That the Article on Legacies and Investments shall not be altered or repealed, except by the vote of two-thirds of the members present at such meeting; and, furthermore, that the quorum necessary for the entertaining of such alterations shall be three-fourths of the entire membership of the Society.

LOUIS ESCHNER
Board of Officers, 1884–1889

FORM OF BEQUEST.

I give and bequeath to the Hebrew Education Society of Philadelphia.

JACOB MAYER
Board of Officers, 1855—1863

The fringe of Jewish population along the northeastern boundary of the city continued to grow, and a colony of Russian immigrants existed there with all the customs, observances and habits of the mother country. The Education Society opened a school on December 28, 1879, at 624 Wayne street, in that part of the city known as "Port Richmond." The school in the B'nai Israel Synagogue was removed to 417 Pine street, and another was opened at Fourth and Poplar streets. The educational advantages that were offered were quickly taken advantage of, and so many attended these schools that they soon became overcrowded, and larger quarters had to be provided.

Although many Israelites had settled at Port Richmond about the year 1876, the "great exodus" was yet to come. The persecution of the Jews in Russia caused thousands to shake the dust from off their feet and seek a land where they could worship their God as their conscience dictated. The first great wave of Russian immigration reached our shores in 1882, and the influx has continued ever since.

JACOB BAMBERGER

The school at No. 624 Wayne street, Port Richmond, was soon found to be too small to meet the demands of the growing population. The properties, Nos. 2856-58 Lark street, a

Rev. Dr. SABATO MORAIS
Board of Officers, 1861–1874
Professor Maimonides College
(Biblical Exegesis)

stone's throw from the Wayne Street School, were secured and entirely remodeled for the use of the Society. The buildings were dedicated on Sunday afternoon, September 16, 1883. The list of those who contributed towards paying for the Industrial School on Lark street, will be found in the appendix. Even these buildings were found inadequate to meet the demands made upon them, and the adjoining property, No. 2854 Lark street, was therefore purchased.

M. A. MITCHELL.
Board of Officers, 1854—1863
" " " 1865—1867
" " " 1869—1871

The first industrial school of the Society was opened in October, 1880, on Wayne street. At first it was a school for girls only. Mrs. Simeon Newhouse was the first superintendent, and she was succeeded in 1881 by Miss Rose Kaufman, and the year following by Mrs. Eva Coons. In 1883 a complete system of industrial education was inaugurated. The most approved method of cigar-making was taught to the men, and joinery, wood-turning and general carpentering were soon added to the course. The department of cigar-manufacturing was opened at the suggestion of Mr. A. M. Frechie, who devoted much time and attention to it. The progress made by the pupils was rapid. The trade-school was soon turning out youths, well equipped in the handicraft they had chosen as a means of livelihood.

SOLOMON TELLER.
Board of Officers, 1856—1859
" " " 1862—1867

In 1886 an industrial school was opened in the Seventh street building, and the course in manual training was extended by the addition of iron-filing.

JUDAH TOURO

chipping, frame making and garment cutting. Thirty boys received instruction in the cigar factory this year (1886). Of these, twenty-five obtained employment at satisfactory wages.

A. MAILERT
Board of Officers, 1864—1867

The teaching of Hebrew still continued. The President of the Society, Mr. Isaac Rosskam, reported that "more children are now being taught the Hebrew language in this city, or are engaged in the study of Hebrew, than ever before."

In 1888 the attendance at the manual training department of the Lark Street School averaged 22; at the school of the same description (technical) at Seventh and Wood streets, 168 pupils were admitted, of which number 152 resided south of Spruce street; 102 were in the cigar department, 56 were being taught garment cutting, and 10 received instruction in carpentry.

The "Young Women's Union, a branch of the Hebrew Education Society," was projected at a meeting held on February 5, 1885. Its main purpose was the education of the poor children of Russian parentage, then so thickly congregated in the southern portion of our city. The Young Women's Union is, also, a product of the great exodus of 1882. It was organized in 1885, chiefly through the efforts of a small number of young women who appreciated the field of labor thus opened to them. The first officers of the Union were: Miss Fanny Binswanger (who first projected the formation of such a society), president; Miss Tinie Feustman, vice-president; Miss Amelia J. Allen, treasurer; Miss Martha Goldstein, corresponding secretary; Miss Clara Ostheim, recording secretary. The Young

DR. JUDAH ISAACS
Board of Officers, 1867—1870

Women's Union ceased to be a branch of the Hebrew Education Society in 1897, when it received a charter from the Commonwealth of Pennsylvania, as an independent organization.

The status of the Society at this stage (1890), is graphically presented in the following report of the then President, Moses A. Dropsie, presented to the Annual Meeting on Sunday, March 7, 1890:

To the Members and Donors of the Hebrew Education Society:

The necessity of educating Jewish youth systematically by competent teachers, with adequate means for instruction in Hebrew, had long been agitated in our community. The knowledge of Hebrew was generally imparted by private teachers, most of whom knew but little beyond the rudiments of the language that they endeavored to teach; and the compensation received by them for tuition was so trifling that they were compelled to pursue other avocations in addition for the means of a livelihood.

For these reasons, the knowledge of Hebrew and of the tenets of Judaism possessed by our youth were extremely limited and vague.

In addition, the text-books used for the instruction of youth in the public and private schools were tinctured with the doctrines of Christianity, reflecting, wittingly or unwittingly, the views and sympathies of the authors and compilers.

This is a true picture of Jewish education in our community fifty years ago, and is a correct representation of the condition of every Jewish community in the United States at that time.

The circumstances of the ignorance of our youth as to their religion, and the low ebb of Hebrew education in our midst, were continually deplored, the difficulties were frequently discussed, but no remedy was adopted. At length, a man arose who indicated the mode of solving this intricate problem. That man was Isaac Leeser, who may be termed the pioneer of American Judaism, whose ardent devotion, self-abnegation, inflexible determination and indomitable energy

Rev. GEORGE JACOBS
Board of Officers, 1869—1874
Prof. Maimonides College
(English Literature)

did more for the advancement of Judaism and the elevation of the Jewish character in the United States than any man who previously or has since existed.

Mr. Leeser's solution of the difficulty was by the formation of this Society, which, it is believed, was the first organization in the United States for the promotion of Jewish education.

Mr. Leeser's views were large and expanded; he sought not only to impart instruction in the rudimental branches of Hebrew education, but he planned that the Jewish youth should be taught the highest branches of Hebrew literature and philosophy, combined with a thorough training of collegiate curriculum. He caused the formation of the Hebrew Education Society on March 7, 1847. It was incorporated by the Legislature of Pennsylvania, April 7, 1848. The charter authorized not only the formation of preparatory schools, but also that of a college, with authority to confer degrees.

The preparatory school was opened on April 7, 1851, and was formed on the model of the public schools. The same text books were used and the same course of instruction was pursued, to which was added tuition in Hebrew, Latin, French and German.

In 1853, the late Judah Touro, through the influence of Mr. Leeser, bequeathed to the Society the sum of $20,000, which was received on February 5, 1854, and thereupon the building on Seventh Street, below Callowhill, was bought on May 28, 1854, and adapted for the school.

On October 28, 1867, Maimonides College was opened under the auspices of the Society. Its design was to impart to its students a thorough education in Hebrew and some of its cognate languages, combined with Biblical and Talmudical lore, and also with the "humanities," so as to fit them for the rabbinate.

The Rev. Isaac Leeser, the Rev. Dr. M. Jastrow, the Rev. Dr. Bettelheim, and the Rev. S. Morais tendered their services gratuitously as professors in the different branches of Jewish learning, which were gratefully accepted.

The expenses incident to the education and support of the students were greater than Philadelphia alone could defray without difficulty, and the contributions of money from New York, which were promised, not being forthcoming, the college ceased to exist.

The preparatory school was of a high order of excellence, and compared favorably with the best of its rank, notwithstanding which some of our people of advanced thought, but not of advanced education, objected to it for the reason that it was sectarian, the answer to which was, that it was open to all, irrespective of creed, that several of its teachers were not Jews, and among its pupils were some who were not Jews.

Another objection urged was, that the pupils of the school lost the opportunity of being admitted into the High School, when properly qualified, as only pupils of the public schools were eligible for admission into that institution. Application was made to the Legislature of Pennsylvania, which by a special law, placed the pupils of the Hebrew Education Society's School on the same footing as that of the public schools, a privilege not granted or possessed by any private school. Thus this objection was silenced.

About the year 1876 a number of Russian Jewish immigrants settled in the northeastern section of the city, then on the extreme boundary of the populated parts, about three and one-fourth miles from the centre of the city, and in a locality distant from the residences or places of business of our co-religionists. The locality was ill-chosen and lacked the essentials for a proper residence; its only advantage was the cheapness of its houses. On the Society being informed of this colony, they deemed it their duty to provide for its educational and moral wants. It opened on December 28, 1879, a school for its instruction, and subsequently bought three adjoining houses, in which it established schools not only for the mental education of its youth, but also for their manual training, teaching the females sewing, knitting, etc., and the males segarmaking, carpentering, etc.

Owing to lack of interest and support, the Society was compelled to abandon its general preparatory school, and to limit its efforts to the teaching of Hebrew and its translation into English, and of Biblical instruction, etc. For this purpose, it has established three schools in different sections of the city. The manual training school in the northeastern section continues, showing good practical results. The Society had established a more extensive manual training school in its hall on Seventh Street, but, owing to its sale, and another proper locality not yet having been obtained, that school is temporarily suspended.

Owing to the severe oppression suffered by our co-religionists in Russia, about the year 1882, a great exodus took place; thousands abandoned or were driven out of their birthplaces and homes, and sought our country as a refuge and as a haven, where they might enjoy that freedom which our institutions confer on every human being. Upon the advent of the van of these immigrants, thousands continued to flow into our land; their number has become so great that they have peopled not only the large cities, but there is scarcely a village or hamlet in the land that does not contain a representative of the Slavic-Jewish race. Russians, Poles, Roumanians and Hungarians now abound everywhere.

These immigrants were received by our co-religionists kindly and affectionately, especially in Philadelphia, where extraordinary efforts were invoked for the amelioration of their condition and where public sentiment was aroused against their oppressors.

This great increase of a necessitous Jewish population has created a corresponding increase of new and greater burdens on the older Jewish population of this city. These immigrants do not speak our language, are unfamiliar with our manners and customs, and were born and reared in a country surrounded by an ignorant and unenlightened population. They came poor and helpless, unaided and alone; they were unable to fight the new battles that they had to contend with. It soon became apparent that, after caring for their physical wants, that mental and physical education were primary factors affecting their circumstances, and the means of absorbing this incongruous mass into the body politic and adapting them to become citizens and performing their duties and obligations in accord with the laws, customs and manners of our civilized society.

The increase of the Jewish population in the United States during the last forty years has been prodigious. The Rev. Isaac Leeser, who probably had a better knowledge respecting the Jews in the United States, and their number, than any other man, when he wrote a brief chapter on this population in No. III of the *Jewish Miscellany*, published by the Philadelphia Jewish Publication Society in 5006, (1846), says: "The number of Jews in the city of New York is said to be about 10,000." From estimates based on a computation made about a dozen years since, and on the increase of immigration and births, and deducting the loss by death, it would seem that the Jewish population of New York at present is about 80,000, an enormous increase in forty years! The patriotic pride of our New York co-religionists claims even a greater population than the number here given.

In the same publication Mr. Leeser states that, "There are now three congregations in Philadelphia, numbering about from 1,500 to 1,800 souls." The Jewish population was then probably about 2,500.

An estimate of the Jewish population in Philadelphia at the present time has been made on data gathered from the membership and seat-holders of the congregations, the membership of the charitable and other societies, clubs, etc. From these statistics it is computed that there are from 26,000 to 28,000 Jews in our city. Of this number about 10,000 were born in Slavic and in Hungarian countries. This large population has settled in our midst within the last twelve years, their necessities have made great and increased demands on the Jewish charitable and educational institutions, and though many of that population have succeeded in becoming self-supporting, yet but very few of them are able to contribute or do contribute in relieving the necessities and caring for the well-being of their countrymen. It is a matter of gratulation that our Jewish community, faithful to the principles of Judaism are practically applying them in the relief of the wants, the amelioration of the condition, and the mental and physical education of these immigrants. To accomplish these objects a large number of Jewesses have volunteered their services, and give time, attention, care and thought, with a devotion and self-denial worthy of the holy cause in which they are engaged.

The Young Men's Hebrew Association have also been working to the same end, and have resolved to extend and widen the field of their labors, but at present lack the proper facilities for systematic and thorough work. Unlike the city of New York, this population is not crowded into one locality; it is somewhat distributed over the city, into what might be termed "clusters;" yet by far the greater bulk of it is located in the territory between South Street and Washington Avenue, and Second and Tenth Streets, a territory of one-half mile north and south, and two-thirds of a mile east and west. Within this territory, the Sunday-school Society has established its schools; the Young Women's Union, which was formed in 1885, has located its Kindergarten and a school for teaching kitchen work and housekeeping, under the auspices of the Hebrew Education Society. The ladies forming this organization are producing excellent results. There have been continual complaints of the want of proper halls and rooms for the uses above mentioned. The increasing population has grown beyond the means afforded for the efficient performance of the necessary work, besides which the sanitary condition of the rooms and auxiliaries is not of a proper character. These evils, though long deplored, are not easily remedied.

It is proposed to secure a plot of land on which to erect a hall that should be surrounded with an abundance of light and air, the hall to have rooms capable of accommodating 1,500 Sunday-school children at one time. It will have rooms for the Young Women's Union and Kindergarten; it will have a room for lectures and a library, and it will also contain ample space for the manual training of females and males. It is also proposed to have baths for females and males, a primary want.

Mention has been made of the work of the Young Men's Hebrew Association. In the erection of the building, regard will be shown to its wants, in furnishing lectures and entertainments of musical, social and amusing character, and in the establishment of an employment and intelligence bureau, where information can be furnished of matters which are essential to the Jewish population.

It is proposed to extend the sphere of manual training, especially in regard to females, by teaching them such handiwork as is adapted to their peculiar skill such as mantua-making, millinery, drafting and cutting of garments, phonographic reporting, typewriting, etc. By the aid of steam-power, the trades that heretofore have been taught will be increased in number. In brief, our aim is to form an institution which will contribute more to the education and elevation of the newly-arrived immigrant than the present system and means afford. We propose to erect an institution in which he will feel he has an interest, and with pride and gratitude recognize the philanthrophy that cares for him, and thus be stimulated to raise himself to the dignity of a freeman, conscious that, as a member of our great Republic, he should

TOURO HALL—HEBREW EDUCATION SOCIETY. Tenth and Carpenter Streets.

strive by his acts and deportment to prove his appreciation of American citizenship.

The Hebrew Education Society, by the erection of the proposed building, and the uses to which it is to be applied, is not prompted solely for the welfare of Jews alone; its benevolence and beneficence are not circumscribed by the narrow boundaries that divide mankind into races and sects. Remembering the Divine command given to our ancestors, "Love thy neighbor as thyself," there will be inscribed on the outer walls of their hall the legend, "Free to all, regardless of creed or color."

Our Society is entering on a new career, and the accomplishment of its aims will leave its impress on our community long after we have passed away.

MOSES A. DROPSIE,
President.

In 1890 a plot of ground was purchased at the southwest corner of Tenth and Carpenter streets, for the sum of twelve thousand dollars. It was proposed to erect thereupon an edifice that would be perfectly adapted to the needs of the Society and of kindred organizations. A Building Fund was organized to which the Jews of Philadelphia responded with unprecedented generosity. The names of those who contributed to this fund will be found in the appendix. The cost of erecting the building was thirty thousand and four hundred dollars, and much more was spent for heating apparatus and furnishing. The total expenditure was over fifty thousand dollars. The architect was Mr. William H. Decker, and Mr. Philip H. Somerset, the builder. The building is a substantial edifice built of red brick trimmed with granite. To honor the memory of an early benefactor of the Society, and of a man eminent as a philanthropist, this splendid structure was named Touro Hall. The corner-stone was laid on Tuesday afternoon, September 22, 1891. Perhaps the most interesting document deposited therein was a history of the Society written in Hebrew by the Rev. Dr. Sabato Morais, giving an account of its rise, organization, progress and work. The dedication took place on November, 27, 1891,—the day set apart by the President of the United States as a day of Thanksgiving. The President, Moses A. Dropsie, Esq., delivered an address, in which he outlined the work of the Society and the great good about to be accomplished. Dr. Morais offered the dedicatory prayer; music was furnished by the orchestra of the Young Men's Hebrew Association; a choir of children sang the concluding hymn. "My Country, 'tis of thee." The services were brief and impressive.

DANIEL GANS
Board of Officers, 1865—1867

A full report of the proceedings on these interesting occasions is quoted from the Report of the 44th Annual Meeting, held March 13, 1892.

At the last Annual Meeting of the Society the members were informed that a plot of ground, 77 feet on Carpenter Street, Tenth Street 87.1½ feet and Paschal Street, 89.7 feet, had been purchased at the southwest corner of Tenth and Carpenter Streets for the sum of $12,000. In March of last year, a contract was made with Philip H. Somerset to erect the building according to plans and specifications furnished by William H. Decker, architect, for the sum of $30,400; and with the Onderdonk Steam-heating and Ventilating Company to heat the building for the sum of $4,637. The cost of erecting the building, including the architect's charges, was $36,249.92, the cost of the ground was $12,000, and sundry charges $700, making a total of $48,949.92.

DAVID TELLER
Board of Officers, 1867–1868

CORNER-STONE.

On Tuesday afternoon, September 22d, 1891, the President deposited a copper box in the corner-stone.

The following documents were contained therein:

Rev. Isaac Leeser's address on the opening of the Society's first school April 1, 1851, presented by Mrs. Judith Solis Cohen.

Reports of the Hebrew Education Society and Young Women's Union, Charter and By-Laws, also a history of the Society, written in Hebrew, by the Rev. Dr. Sabato Morais, giving an account of its origin, progress and work, together with a list of names composing the present Board of Officers.

Reports of Jewish Hospital Association, including the ceremonies at laying the corner-stone of the Hospital, the corner-stone of the New Home and the dedication of the New Home.

Report of the Jewish Foster Home and Asylum, also Constitution and By-Laws.

Report of the United Hebrew Charities, 1891.

Report of the Fiftieth Anniversary of the Hebrew Sunday-school Society, Programme of the Fifty-third Anniversary, Constitution and By-Laws, 1858 and 1891.

List of patrons and members Young Men's Hebrew Association, prospectus for 1890-91. Constitution and By-Laws.

Report of the Committee of Arrangements for the corner-stone of the Synagogue of the Congregation Mikvé Israel, 1859, Charter and Constitution and By-Laws, 1824 and 1884. List of present members.

Constitution and By-Laws Congregation Rodef Shalom, 1867.

List of the first officers and present officers and members of Congregation Beth Israel.

Report of Congregation Keneseth Israel, 1891.

The Jews in Philadelphia prior to 1800, by Hyman P. Rosenbach.

Statistics of the Jews of the United States, by Wm. B. Hackenburg, 1880.

Reports of Hebrew Immigrants' Aid Society, 1882 to 1891.

Prospectus of the Jewish Maternity Association and Seventh Annual Report of the Society Ezrath Nashim.

Reports of the Jewish Theological Seminary, 1888 and 1890.

Report of Grand Lodge Kesher Shel Barzel, 1891.

Report of the Jewish Publication Society and an account of the persecution of the Jews in Russia, published by the Society.

Report of Orphans' Guardian Society, 1891.

List of names of officers of the Female Hebrew Benevolent Society.

Reports of the Alliance Israélite Universelle.

Discourse delivered in the Synagogue Rodef Shalom, November 24, 1864, panegyric of the Rev. Isaac Leeser, and a sketch of the Alliance Israélite Universelle, by Moses A. Dropsie, Esq.

Oration delivered by David Solis Cohen, on the centennial anniversary birthday of Sir Moses Montefiore, at Portland, Or.

The Dayatouns, by Henry S. Morais.

The Occident, January, 1869, containing an article on the Talmud, by Emanuel Deutsch.

Inaugural report and plan of action of Jewish Alliance of America.

Catalogue of the Leeser Library, and a report of the Oriental Antiquities in the United States National Museum, by Dr. Cyrus Adler.

Memorial of Isidor Binswanger, a former President of the Society.

Report of the first and second annual charity dinner in Philadelphia, 1853 and 1854.

Ten copies of the *Public Ledger*, containing the History of the Jews of Philadelphia, by Henry S. Morais.

Daily Papers.

Jewish weekly papers, *Jewish Exponent, American Hebrew, Jewish Messenger* and *American Israelite*.

List of names of subscribers to the Building Fund.

DEDICATION.

The dedication of the building took place on Thursday afternoon, November 27th (Thanksgiving Day) 1891. The exercises commenced with the Priest's March, from Mendelssohn's "Athalie," performed by the orchestra of the Young Men's Hebrew Association, directed by Mr. Marcus Lewin. A hymn in Hebrew was sung by the children of the Sunday-school, directed by Mr. Samuel Jacobs, with Mr. Bowers as organist. Next followed an address by the President, Moses A. Dropsie, Esq., who was followed by Rev. Dr. S. Morais, with the Dedicatory Prayer. The Children's Choir then sang "My Country, 'tis of thee," which concluded the exercises. The thanks of the Society are due to all who so kindly assisting, made the occasion such a pleasant and successful one. The Reception Committee consisted of the following gentlemen:

CLINTON O. MAYER, *Chairman*. SAMUEL JACOBS.
OSCAR B. TELLER. ADOLPH EICHHOLZ.
DAVID W. AMRAM. DAVID KIRSCHBAUM.
WILLIAM B. ROSSKAM. MAX HERZBERG.
WALTER S. GANS. DAVID MANDEL, JR.
FRANK BACHMAN. EPHRAIM LEDERER.
ARTHUR S. ARNOLD. BERNARD HARRIS.

FIRST SESSION HELD.

The first school session was held in the building on Monday, December 14th, up to which time the work had been carried on at 522 Bainbridge Street; this building has since been sub-let to the Hebrew Literature Society, an organization consisting entirely of Russians, and has been in existence for the last seven years, which continues that part of our labors formerly carried on by the Young Men's Hebrew Association, the latter taking charge of the Reading room, Library, Lectures and Entertainments in the new building.

HOW THE BUILDING IS BEING OCCUPIED.

The building is occupied by the Sunday-school (with 650 pupils) and Sewing-school (with 285 pupils), of the Hebrew Sunday-school Society.

The Agent of the Immigration Society.

The Auxiliary Charities having in charge the dispensing of the Baron de Hirsch Trust and Employment Bureau.

Hebrew School.

Night School, English branches.

Tin-smithing School.

Dress-making School.

Carpentry School.

The dimensions of the bathing-pool are 14 x 38.6 feet, with a depth ranging from 4 to 5 feet.

SUBSCRIPTIONS TO THE BUILDING.

The amount subscribed to the Building Fund to date.	$30,364 00
Of this amount $1,815.84 was received from the Hebrew Sunday-school Society.	
The subscriptions to the Furniture Fund amounted to	2,660 00
Making a total, ...	$33,024 00

The officers of the Hebrew Education Society during the eventful year in which was consummated the fond desires of many of its former workers, were Moses A. Dropsie, president; Isaac Rosskam, vice-president; Gabriel Blum, treasurer, and David Sulzberger, honorary secretary.

THEODORE MINDEL.
Board of Officers, 1868-1874.

The first school session in the new building was held on Monday, December 14, 1891, and from this date the work of the Society has gone on with a full measure of success. A year after the opening of Touro Hall, 1345 pupils had been admitted into the Hebrew course, 919 in the course in English and 164 in the cigar-making department. A night school was established in order to accommodate those who were unable to attend during the day. The financial condition of the Society was fairly prosperous, and the membership roll was increased.

Miss Ellen Phillips, whose demise took place on February 2, 1891, and who had been for many years interested in the success of the Hebrew Education Society, bequeathed to it the sum of fifteen thousand dollars. A bronze tablet erected in her memory was placed in the main hall.

It bears this inscription: "In memory of Miss Ellen Phillips, a kind friend and generous benefactor of the Society.

MISS ELLEN PHILLIPS

TRUSTEES OF BARON DE HIRSCH FUND.

Her unstinted and unsectarian charity and long continued labor in the religious education of youth, add her name to the distinguished roll of the women of Israel who have enobled humanity."

THE PRINCIPAL BENEFICIARIES.

The industrial and general education which the Society is disseminating among the Russian refugees settled in this city and in which special direction over five thousand dollars of its income is expended, has been furthered since September, 1892, by the allotment of twenty-four hundred dollars per annum accorded to this Society from the Baron de Hirsch Fund.

DAVID AARON
Board of Officers, 1871—1876

Thus the Hebrew Education Society has become the local agency for the educational work of the great charity organized in this country for the benefit of the Russian and Roumanian Jews, by the late Baron Maurice de Hirsch.

This foundation was established by a special deed of trust, executed March 1, 1890, and was committed to a Board of Trustees, with headquarters in New York.

The original committee was composed as follows: Hon. Mayer S. Isaacs, President; Jacob H. Schiff, Vice-President; Dr. Julius Goldman, Secretary; Emanuel Lehman, Treasurer; Hon. Oscar S. Straus, Jesse Seligman, Henry Rice and James H. Hoffman of New York, and Hon. Mayer Sulzberger and Wm. B. Hackenburg of Philadelphia; Hon. A. S. Solomon, General Agent of the Foundation.

HERMAN VAN BEIL
Charter Member
Board of Officers, 1848—1849

The Hon. Oscar S. Straus and Dr. Goldman have resigned

from the Committee, and Jesse Seligman died. Mr. Abraham Abraham has since been added to the Board.

The capital amounts to two million and five hundred thousand dollars, and the income therefrom is about one hundred thousand dollars per annum; sixty per cent. of this is intended for educational purposes, and from this source is the annual contribution of twenty-four hundred dollars to the Hebrew Education Society obtained.

The Committee have established English schools and Trade Schools in New York, and an Agricultural and Industrial School at Woodbine, New Jersey. The forty per cent. is used to assist industrial immigrants by furnishing them with tools, and if necessary with loans, upon farms they have themselves acquired and demonstrated their ability to work to advantage, etc. The Philadelphia office is conducted by the Auxiliary Branch of the United Hebrew Charities (in Touro Hall.)

SIMON ELFELT.
Charter Member
Vice President, 1848
Board of Officers, 1848—1850.

BARON MAURICE DE HIRSCH.

The Trust co-operates with existing philanthropic institutions in various places.

Mrs. ROSANNA OSTERMAN

Baron Maurice de Hirsch died in Paris in May, 1896, and the deplorable event was made the occasion of a special meeting of the Board of Officers, at which the following resolution was adopted:

"In solemn resignation to the Divine will, this Society mourns the death of Baron Maurice de Hirsch as that of the noblest philanthropist of modern times and as that of a man who has afforded, not only to Israel, but to all mankind, one of the most signal examples of devotion to his suffering brethren that history has recorded.

"As almoners of a part of the world-wide benefactions which Baron de Hirsch had instituted during his lifetime, the Hebrew Education Society of Philadelphia has special occasion to testify to the grandeur of his undertaking for the benefit of his suffering co-religionists in this land of their refuge as well as in the lands of their oppression. Here, as elsewhere in the broad expanse of Baron de Hirsch's charity, the foundation of his beneficence has been laid by him on the grand work of education and enlightenment, and these great factors of moral and material well-being he has strengthened by a far-seeing provision for the permanent

ABRAHAM SUSSMAN

elevation of the suffering victims of oppression through aiding them to self-maintenance. Thus founded the charity which he has extended to the multitude of his beneficiaries, has become an unmixed good, and thereby his vast munificence has been made a blessing to them and to their posterity.

"The generous bounty and far-reaching benevolence of Baron Maurice de Hirsch will find in the elevation and future development of the Russian Jews in America, both in the Northern and Southern continents, a living monument that is destined to be as lasting as the history of civilization."

(Signed) ISAAC ROSSKAM, *President.*
D. SULZBERGER, *Secretary.*

MRS. MINNIE K. ARNOLD
Board of Officers, 1896—1898

An engrossed copy of the above, suitably bound in the form of a volume, was forwarded to the widowed Baroness De Hirsch, its receipt eliciting the following acknowledgements:

2 Rue de l'Elysee,
PARIS, July 30, 1896.
The Secretary to the Hebrew Education Society in Philadelphia:

DEAR SIR,—I am greatly obliged to you for forwarding me the resolutions of your Board, and beg of you to convey to the members of the Board my heartfelt appreciation of their thoughtful kindness.

Yours truly,
BARONESS DE HIRSCH-GEREUTH.

2 Rue de l'Elysee,
PARIS, August 7, 1896.
To the Board of Officers of the Hebrew Education Society in Philadelphia:

MORRIS C. LICHTEN
Board of Officers, 1882—1884

GENTLEMEN,—I am in possession of the minute adopted in the meeting of your Board on the 10th of May last to take action on the death of the late Baron Maurice de Hirsch, which you forwarded to

BARONESS CLARA DE HIRSCH-GEREUTH.

me in so handsome and tasteful a form. I was deeply touched by the feelings of thankfulness and admiration set forth therein towards my regretted husband, and I wish to thank you and to express my heartfelt appreciation of this token of thoughtful kindness on your part.

Yours very truly, BARONESS DE HIRSCH GEREUTH.*

The erection of Touro Hall, and its complete and thorough equipment for its great educational purpose, naturally resulted in soon making the establishment a centre of intellectual activity. This development has manifested itself in many different ways, such as the formation, tentatively it is true, of a class in higher Hebrew as in a measure preparatory for the

ISIDORE COONS
Board of Officers, 1885–1886
Vice-President, 1886–1891

courses of the newly founded Gratz College, and the arrangement and delivery of a series of University Extension Lectures. The condition of this movement cannot better be indicated than by a citation of the letter from the Secretary of

*Reference to the death of the Baroness de Hirsch will be found included in the appended Fifty-first Annual Report, March, 1899.

the University Extension Society, as communicated to the Secretary of the Education Society and which we quote in full, as follows:

Mrs. HORACE A. NATHANS
Board of Officers, 1894—

PHILADELPHIA, February 9, 1894.

My Dear Sir:

I beg to report that the six lecture courses on Civics, arranged originally between Mr. Walter Vrooman and myself, on behalf of the Society, was delivered at Touro Hall on the following dates: September 28, October 5, 12, 17, 24 and 31. Permission to use the hall was very kindly given by the Hebrew Education Society, through yourself. It was originally expected that there would be in attendance a large number of those not in any way connected with the school held under the auspices of the Hebrew Education Society, and Mr. Vrooman expressed great confidence in his ability to secure an audience that would entirely fill the lecture room placed by the Society at our disposal. His expectations in this respect were not realized, so that the course was really given to the older students of your own evening school. This of itself, however, made an excellent audience and one that was no doubt better prepared for the instruction given than a more general audience would have been.

I have to report the closest attention to the lectures, and a wide-awake intelligent interest in the subjects discussed. Several students passed the examination successfully. The conditions of issuing certificates were that an essay should be written at some time while the course was in progress, on some one of the subjects assigned, these conditions having been several times clearly stated to the students.

PHILIP LEWIN
Board of Officers, 1886—1894

The names of those who received certificates are Morris Josephson, Joseph I. Komarovski, Julius H. Komarovski and Joseph Katz.

In conclusion allow me to say that the conditions at Touro Hall seem excellent for University Extension work, and that it is my strong conviction that if a canvass were properly made, in the ordinary University Extension manner, an audience could be found that would fill the lecture room. The limited attendance to which reference is made above, probably resulted from an attempt to bring the audience too great a distance, and from a lack of familiarity with University Extension methods.

Trusting that you will command my services whenever I can be of any assistance, I am

Very cordially yours,
EDWARD T. DEVINE,
Lecturer.

To Mr. DAVID SULZBERGER.

Mrs. FLORENCE K. LIVERIGHT
Board of Officers, 1892–1895
1897—

In the following Fall season another University Extension course was organized and six lectures were delivered, beginning in November, 1894, and ending in January, 1895. Regarding this course, it is cited in the Annual Report for 1895, that "the lecturer, Mr. Cheesman A. Herrick, was enabled by his distinct and clear enunciation to hold the attention of his audience. The 'talk' at the close of the lecture was invariably instructive and interesting.

The subject, American History, was comprised under the following heads:

I. Discovery and Early Settlement of America.
II. Colonial History.
III. Revolutionary War.
IV. The Constitution.
V. National Development.
VI. Our Great Civil War.

HENRY GERSTLEY
Board of Officers, 1889–1891

In an article which appeared in the University Extension

Journal, August, 1894, written by Frank S. Edmonds, he shows in a table of statistics that there were thirty-two classes in the University Extension of Philadelphia, with a total attendance of 2095; certificates granted, 46; of these ten were given to those who attended the lectures at the Hebrew Literature Society, 322 Bainbridge street, and four to those who attended at Touro Hall."

Mrs. H. S. LOUCHHEIM
Board of Officers, 1895——

The outcome of this enterprise is briefly stated in the President's Report, at the annual meeting on March 8, 1896, from which it appears that "the question of University Extension was considered by the Board of Officers, and was debated at considerable length. It was, however, eventually decided that while the lectures had been measurably successful and advantageous, it necessarily shortened the hours of instruction in the entire school, while but a small portion of the pupils understood the lecturer or were benefited thereby; furthermore, it was stated that Ephraim Lederer, Esq., intended continuing his lectures on the Constitution as heretofore, all of which would take away too much time from the regular course of instruction, more especially since the Young Men's Hebrew Association has furnished a series of entertainments and a course of lectures during the entire winter of 1895 and the spring of 1896."

SOL. L. HAAS
Treasurer, 1883
Board of Officers, 1889—1890

Two other courses of lectures were delivered, the one on the "Victorian Poets," and the other on the "English Novelists."

Those on the "Victorian Poets" were delivered by Dr. Frederick H. Sykes, on October 28, November 4 and 11, 1897; the subjects were Alfred Tennyson, Alfred Austin and Rudyard Kipling. The average attendance, 156.

The "English Novelists" series was delivered by Mr. Clyde Furst, on January 27, February 3, 10 and 17, 1898; the subjects being Sir Walter Scott, William Makepeace Thackeray and Charles Dickens, with an average attendance of 149.

Mrs. EVA COONS
Board of Officers, 1897——

In 1895, on the occasion of the high holiday season, a free synagogue for the benefit of the large Jewish population in the district around Touro Hall, was inaugurated in that building. This assembly has been continued during the holidays since its first organization, the arrangements being now under the direct control of the Society.

These free services have proven attractive to the worshippers and generally satisfactory. The excellent personnel of the congregations which assemble, the notable dignity and decorum of the service and the general circumstances attending the occasions, all point to the great desirability of establishing these free services on a permanent basis.

The educational value, the elevating influence and the far-reaching significance of such services, properly established and controlled, cannot but be apparent to those who are conversant with the existing conditions among our Russo-Jewish brethren in the southern section of the city.

ANDREW KAAS
Board of Officers, 1897——

At the meeting of the Board, held April 19, 1889, the Secretary reported the following correspondence between himself and Rev. Dr. S. Morais.

PHILADELPHIA, April 18, 1889.

REV. DR. S. MORAIS,
President Theological Seminary.

Dear Sir:

It was brought to the notice of the Board of Officers of the Hebrew Education Society that a number of Hebrew books donated to the Society some time ago were in a bad condition and would cost considerable to put into such shape as to make them available. On motion the Secretary was requested to make the best possible disposition of them. Being a legacy, the books cannot be given away, but by the authority conferred on me by the resolution I have determined to have them bound at my own expense and loan them to the Theological Seminary, until such time as the Board of Officers or the Society may desire that they be returned.

To which the following reply was received:

DAVID SULZBERGER, ESQ.,

Dear Sir:

In the name of the Jewish Theological Seminary Association I thank you for having had the Hebrew books, to which you have reference, bound at your own expense, and through you I beg to thank the officers of the Hebrew Education Society for their offer to let the pupils of said institution have the use thereof for an indeterminate time.

April 19, 1889.   Yours very respectfully,   S. MORAIS.

Pursuant to the above the following books were sent to the Theological Seminary of New York.

TALMUD—Gittin, Chulin, Yebamoth, Rosh Ha Shanah, Pesachim, Shabath, Berachoth, Baba Batra, Baba Kama, Nidah, Erubin, Zebachim, Menachot, Synhedrin.

SHULCHAN ARUCH—Eben Ha Ezer, Chosen Mishpot, Orach Chayim.

Shaloth v. Tishuboth, Mate Dan, En Yaacob.

The Technical School of the B'nai B'rith was removed from its former location in Pine street, to Touro Hall in January, 1897, the Society having made special provision for its accomodation. A record of this proceeding is afforded by the correspondence relating to it, which is here appended:

PHILADELPHIA, Dec. 11, 1896.

Benjamin Wolf, Esq., President pro tem. of the Hebrew Education Society:

At the stated meeting of the Governing Committee of the B'nai B'rith Manual Training School held last evening the following motion was adopted unanimously:

GEORGE WIENER
Board of Officers, 1887–1890

That the Governing Committee of the Manual Training School apply to the Board of Directors of the Hebrew Education Society for space in its building in which to pursue the work of the B'nai B'rith Manual Training School and that a committee of three be appointed to confer with a similar committee of your Board of Directors to perfect the necessary arrangements.

The committee appointed by the Governing Committee of the Manual Training School are Brothers H. S. Friedman, Charles Hoffman and Jacob Singer.

Kindly inform me of your action.

Submitting this for your kind consideration, by order of the Governing Committee of the M. T. S.

Very truly yours,
M. K. COHEN, *Secretary,*
2425 Camac Place.

To this the following reply was forwarded:

SIMON FLEISHER
Board of Officers, 1887–1893

PHILADELPHIA, Dec. 15, 1896.

To the Committee of the Manual Training School of the Independent Order of B'nai B'rith:

GENTLEMEN,—Your communication in regard to your school

was considered at a stated meeting of the Board of Officers of the Hebrew Education Society, held on Sunday last, the 13th inst., when a resolution was adopted authorizing the Industrial and Hall Committees to grant the use of such rooms in Touro Hall as may be required for your classes.

The committees are desirous of aiding in furthering the work which, up to the present time, has been so ably conducted by you and assure you of their cheerful co-operation and shall be pleased to meet you either this evening, to-morrow evening or Thursday evening to arrange the necessary details, I am, Most respectfully yours,

D. SULZBERGER,
Chairman Hall Com.

GABRIEL BLUM
Treasurer, 1891 — —

On February 3, 1897, the Governing Committee of the B'nai B'rith Manual Training School held a meeting in Touro Hall, and directed to the Board of Officers the following communication:

PHILADELPHIA, February 10, 1897.
David Sulzberger, Secretary Hebrew Education Society:

DEAR SIR :—At the last meeting of the Governing Committee of the B'nai B'rith Manual Training School, held on February 3, 1897, I was requested to say to you that in accordance with the arrange-

HEBREW EDUCATION SOCIETY.

ments made between the committee of your Board of Directors and a like number of our Governing Committee, the kind offer you extended to us in granting sufficient room in your building for our Manual Training School has been accepted, and we are now occupying the space alloted to us.

The thanks of the Governing Committee of the B'nai B'rith Manual Training School is hereby tendered to the Hebrew Education Society, which, through the Board of Directors, is ever ready to promote the interest of education among Israelites. Your aid and assistance otherwise extended to our cause is also accepted and will be gratefully remembered by us.

Trusting that harmony of action may always exist between us, and that our joint efforts may be crowned with the best results,

I remain very truly yours,

M. K. COHEN.

Secretary Governing Committee, B'nai B'rith M. T. S.

MAYER GANS

DAVID HOFFMAN

At the meeting of the Board of Officers, held November 14, 1897, a communication was received from Moses A. Dropsie, President of the Board of Trustees of Gratz College, asking for rooms in Touro Hall for the purpose of the College. Three rooms were prepared and the free use of them granted for the classes which were instructed by Mess. Speaker, Dembitz and Husik. The College was opened on January 3, 1898, the classes instructed by Mess. Dembitz and Husik were opened January 6. Instruction in Mr. Speaker's class did not begin until January 25.

In reviewing the fifty years' work of the Society as recorded in the preceding pages, one important feature of its history may well be dwelt upon.

DR. MORRIS JASTROW, JR.
Board of Officers, 1891–1892

While constantly keeping in view the prime object of the Hebrew Education Society's existence, which is sufficiently indicated in its title, the steadfast policy pursued by the organization during the past twenty years of its activity has been that of keeping its work rigorously within the limits imposed by the means available for the purpose. In this period the Society has constantly aimed to widen its scope and to meet the increasing requirements of its work to the fullest possible extent, but always with such conservation of its forces as would give security to its foundation and permanence to its future.

The decline of the Society's influence and efficiency which developed in the third decade of its existence, and which reached its lowest stage about 1878, was definitely brought about by a neglect of these prime considerations, as is clearly manifest from the various reports of its officers, who sought, as it appears from these reports, to make the Society's school to "excel all others." Laudable as was such ambition, it was undoubtedly ill-advised, as is evidenced by the fact that the entire legacy of Judah Touro, amounting to twenty thousand dollars, instead of being set aside as a source of income, was spent upon the current work and its value as a foundation thus completely destroyed. It is not to be said that the fund

EDWARD WOLF,
Board of Officers, 1891–

was wasted, inasmuch as no little good was accomplished by its use, but the policy thus indicated may justly be considered as more than questionable. This policy has since been reversed, and the By-Laws of the Society have been carefully framed to the end that every legacy be made a permanent fund, and that only its income may be currently used.

Mrs. MATILDA H. COHEN

With the beginning of the present decade, the Society entered a period of comparative and increasing prosperity. In 1891 new classes of membership were organized, including that of regular members paying five dollars per annum, patrons contributing twenty-five dollars and friends one hundred dollars annually, and in 1894 the fee for life membership was increased from one hundred to two hundred and fifty dollars.

In 1879 the report of the Treasurer showed the whole income from membership dues to be $435.00, and from the Permanent Fund (the $2500 estate of Daniel Gans), $150.00 a total of $585.00.

In 1898 the report of the Treasurer shows an income from the like sources of a total of $5425.82, a tenfold increase of resources, enabling a naturally corresponding increase of the Society's activity.

During a period of twenty-seven years, namely from 1851 to 1878, the school of the Society was conducted on the plan of a seminary, giving a

HEZEKIAH ARNOLD
Executor Estate Isaac Leeser

general education to its pupils. In the latter year it was found necessary to abandon this undertaking, and the work of the Society was then restricted to the single direction of instruction in Hebrew. In 1891, however, the Society found itself enabled to extend its efforts in the direction of industrial education, and several trade schools, as well as an English night school, were then instituted. These schools have since been continued and enlarged, and most excellent results have been accomplished in both directions.

The industrial schools have attracted a gratifying number of pupils, many of whom have acquired a degree of proficiency in their respective callings sufficient to enable them to thereby earn a living.

Mrs. BERTHA GANS

Since 1869 the Society has received an annual donation of varying amount from the Charity Ball Fund, and since 1892, a stipend of two hundred dollars per month from the American Baron de Hirsch Fund. These contributions, supplementing the income of the Society from its members, patrons and friends and from its Permanent Fund, have enabled the Society to develop its work to a degree not otherwise possible.

The far-reaching importance of the Society's work can be fully appreciated only by those who have personally visited the various schools while in session, and thus realized that the beneficent work of the Hebrew Education Society accrues to the benefit, not merely of its pupils, but ultimately to the community of which they form a part.

LEOPOLD FURTH

LEGACIES.

In the following list of the Permanent Fund of the Society, it will be found that some of the legacies became operative some time after the death of the testators; that of Mayer Arnold was a contingent bequest, and though he died in 1868, it was not until 1883 that the legacy was paid.

The Sussman legacy was held at Bellefonte for some time, the deceased having willed five hundred dollars for a Hebrew school at that place, but in the event of none being established, the bequest should be paid to the Hebrew Education Society of Philadelphia.

The first payment of interest on this legacy was reported at the meeting of the Board of Officers, held June 6, 1886.

The Guarantee Trust and Safe Deposit Company was custodian of the fund until 1895. At a meeting of the Board of Officers, held on December 8th of that year, it was reported that the legacy of Abraham Sussman had been paid over to the Society by the Guarantee Trust and Safe Deposit Company, pursuant to an order of the Orphan's Court of Centre County at Bellefonte, at a session of the Court held November 25, 1895.

The legacy of $2500 from Daniel Gans was in the hands of his executors, Messrs. Mayer and Aaron Gans, for a period of twenty years. In 1889 Mr. Aaron Gans, the surviving executor, applied to the Orphan's Court to be relieved of the trust, which application was granted; the President became the trustee *ex officio*, with the Society itself as the surety.

The legacy of two hundred dollars from Isaac Leeser only became operative six years after his death, at which time a final settlement of the estate was made.

The amounts bequeathed by Solomon Solis ($200), Rosanna Osterman ($1000), Isaac Leeser ($200) and Jacob Bamberger ($250), amounting to sixteen hundred and fifty dollars, had been applied to the general purposes of the Society; however, through the efforts of the Board of Officers, between the years 1889 and 1891, this amount was recovered into the treasury of the Society.

The Touro legacy of twenty thousand dollars could not so be recovered, but the Board of Officers on the erection of the new building in 1891, at the southwest corner of Tenth and Carpenter streets, named it Touro Hall. This edifice, when completed, cost fifty-two thousand dollars. It is a worthy monument of that great philanthropist.

Permanent Fund.

The Permanent Fund consists of the legacies to the Society since 1854, Life Memberships and the money at interest for Special Prizes.

1854.	Solomon Solis	$ 200 00
1866.	Rosanna Osterman	1,000 00
1869.	Daniel Gans	2,500 00
1874.	Isaac Leeser	200 00
	Jacob Bamberger	250 00
1882.	Abraham Adler	300 00
1883.	Mayer Arnold	100 00
1886.	Mayer Gans	500 00
	Abraham Sussman	500 00
1887.	Rachel Whitzstein (Industrial Fund)	200 00
	Rev. J. Frankel	25 00
1891.	Bertha Gans	250 00
1892.	Ellen Phillips	15,000 00
1894.	Leopold Furth	50 00
	David Hoffman	500 00
1896.	Solomon Gans	500 00
1897.	Morris Sickles	100 00
	Simon Fleisher	1,000 00
	Joseph Rosenbaum	500 00
1898.	Lucien Moss	100 00
1899.	Aaron Lichten	250 00
	Henry Gerstley	1,000 00
	Theresa Loeb	400 00
	Lena Max	100 00

Prize Fund, Industrial School:
Sidney Trieste Memorial for Children   100 00
Sidney Trieste Memorial for Adults   300 00

Prize Fund, Industrial School for Girls:
Matilda H. Cohen Memorial   100 00

Prize Fund, Night School:
Isidore Coons Memorial   100 00

Prize Fund, Kindergarten:
Morton M. Newburger Memorial   100 00

Prize Fund, Arithmetic and Composition:
Aaron Lichten   1,000 00
Life Membership Fund   500 00
    ———
    27,725 00

Names of Officers since the Organization of the Society, 1848-1898.

Presidents.

1848 S. Solis,*
1854 A. S. Wolf,
1862 M. A. Dropsie,
1870 I. Binswanger,
1878 A. Adler,*
1880 Isaac Rosskam,
1889 M. A. Dropsie,
1892 Moyer Fleisher,
1895 Isaac Rosskam,
1898 Benjamin Wolf.

Vice-Presidents.

1848 Simon Elfelt,
1849 A. S. Wolf,
1854 Rev. I. Leeser,
1861 M. A. Dropsie,
1862 A. T. Jones,
1867 Rev. M. Jastrow,
1874 A. Adler,
1878 Isaac Rosskam,
1880 Mayer Sulzberger,
1881 Isaac Saller,
1886 Isidore Coons,
1891 Isaac Rosskam,
1895 Benjamin Wolf,
1898 Ephraim Lederer.

Treasurers.

1848 Abraham Hart,
1875 S. Muhr,
1876 S. B. Fleisher,
1883 Sol. L. Haas,
1883 Levi Mayer,
1891 Gabriel Blum.

Secretaries.

1848 L. M. Klosser,
     Z. A. Davis,
     M. A. Dropsie,
1849 A. I. H. Bernal,
     Rev. I. Leeser,
1850 A. T. Jones,
1854 M. M. Allen,
1857 J. M. Emanuel,
1863 L. M. Allen,
1863 A. M. Frichel,
1864 Edwin W. Arnold,
1866 Dr. J. Solis Cohen,
1868 Aaron Lazarus,
1870 Samuel Hecht,
1874 A. Lichten,
1876 D. Sulzberger.

Asst. Secretaries.

1848 S. M. Klosser,
1849 D. Van Beil,
1851 A. Finzi,
1868 Elis P. Levy,
1873 L. A. Mitchell, (pro tem)
1874 L. A. Mitchell,
1874 H. M. Rosenbaum,
1876 E. L. Rosenbaum,
1877 Louis Gerstley.

None chosen after 1878.

HEBREW EDUCATION SOCIETY.

Board of Officers.

David Aaron,
S. Alexander,
Michael M. Allen,
David W. Amram,
S. Appel,
Edwin Arnold,
Mrs. Minnie K. Arnold,
Mayer Arnold,
Simon W. Arnold,
Maurice Bamberger,
Dr. Aaron S. Bettelheim,
Isidore Binswanger,
Charles Bloomingdale,
S. N. Carvalho,
Marcus Caufman,
Charles J. Cohen,
David S. Cohen,
Jacob Solis Cohen,
Lewis L. Cohen,
Myer D. Cohen,
Mrs. Eva Coons,
Isidore Coons,
Henry Dalsheimer,
Zadoc A. Davis,
H. De Boer,
Moses A. Dropsie,
Joseph Einstein,
Simon Ettele,
Louis Eschner,
Mrs. Samuel Espen,
Joseph Fels,
Benj. W. Fleisher, Jr.,
Monte Fleisher,
Simon B. Fleisher,
Simon Fleisher,
Henry M. Frank,
A. M. Fretchie,
H. Friedberger,
Daniel Gans,
Solomon Gans,
Henry Gerstley,
Louis Gerstley,
William Gerstley,
M. Goldman,
A. Goldsmith,
Mrs. Wm. B. Hackenburg,

Sol. L. Haas,
Abraham Hart,
Lazarus Hecht,
Joseph Hefferon,
Simon Heffer,
Mason Hirsh,
Isaac Hyneman,
Sam'l M. Hyneman,
Dr. Judah Isaacs,
Rev. George Jacobs,
Morris Jastrow, Jr.,
C. Johnson,
Alfred T. Jones,
Andrew Kaas,
Morris Kohn,
Jacob Langsdorf,
L. J. Legerman,
Ephraim Lederer,
Rev. Isaac Leeser,
Louis E. Levy,
Philip Lewin,
Aaron Lichten,
Morris C. Lichten,
Moses H. Lichten,
Mrs. Florence K. Liveright,
Simon Liveright,
Jacob Loeb,
Mrs. H. S. Louchheim,
A. Mailler,
H. Mayer,
Jacob Mayer,
Levi Mayer,
Jacob Miller,
Theodore Mendel,
Henry Mitchell,
M. A. Mitchell,
Rev. Sabato Morais,
Lucien Moss,
Michael Moyer,
Jacob Muhr,
Simon Muhr,
Joseph Newhouse,
Mrs. Horace A. Nathans,
Moses Nathans,
David Pison,
H. Polock,

T. B. POTTSDAMER,
ISAAC ROSSKAM,
WM. B. ROSSKAM,
ED. L. ROTHSCHILD,
ISAAC SALLER,
JOSEPH SCHOENEMAN,
MARK SCHWARTZ,
JOSEPH J. SNELLENBURG,
DAVID H. SOLIS,
JULIUS STERN,
SAMUEL STERNBERGER,
JACOB SULZBERGER,

HON. MAYER SULZBERGER,
DAVID TELLER,
SOLOMON TELLER,
S. THALHEIMER,
A. C. VAN BEIL,
H. VAN BEIL,
GEORGE WIENER,
ABM. S. WOLF,
BENJAMIN WOLF,
EDWARD WOLF,
ELIAS WOLF,
JACOB WOLF.

Officers of the Young Women's Union

From 1886 to 1896.

PRESIDENTS.

1886 MISS FANNY BINSWANGER,   1893 ROSINA FELS,
1896 ALICE E. JASTROW.

VICE-PRESIDENTS.

1886 MRS. EDW'D GOLDSTEIN,   1894 MISS J. FRIEDBERGER,
1887 MISS ROSINA FELS,   1895 MISS ALICE E. JASTROW,
1893 MISS ALICE E. JASTROW,   1896 MISS HELEN FLEISHER.

TREASURERS.

1886 MISS AMELIA J. ALLEN,   1890 MISS ELVIRA N. SOLIS,
1887 MISS TERESA FLEISHER,   1893 MISS AMELIA BISSINGER,
1895 MISS JULIA FRIEDBERGER.

RECORDING SECRETARIES.

1886 MISS CLARA OSTHEIM,   1892 MISS CARRIE E. AMRAM,
1890 MISS ROSA GOLDSMITH,   1893 MISS SARAH WEIL,
1895 MISS LEAH ABELLS.

CORRESPONDING SECRETARIES.

1886 MISS M. GOLDSTEIN,   1890 MISS ADDIE H. TELLER,
1887 MISS GRACE FLEISTMAN,   1892 MISS CLARA POTSDAMER,
1889 MISS AMELIA BISSINGER,   1896 MISS M. FRIEDENWALD.

SUMMARY.

January 27, 1847—Hebrew School Fund Ball.

March 7, 1847—Preliminary meeting held.

June 4, 1848—Constitution and By-Laws adopted.

July 16, 1848—First regular meeting held.

April 7, 1849—Society incorporated.

April 7, 1851—School first opened in Zane (Filbert) street.

October 26, 1851—Plans suggested "in order to raise funds for the benefit of the Society."

    1852—Meeting of Committees of the Society with a committee of the Congregation Rodef Shalom, to consider the advisability of opening an additional Hebrew school.

February 23, 1853—First Charity Dinner.

1854—Solomon Solis, first President of the Society, died (during his incumbency).

    Legacy of Solomon Solis received.

February 2, 1854—Second Charity Dinner.

February 5, 1854—Judah Touro's legacy of $20,000 received.

May 28, 1854—Purchase of Seventh street school house authorized.

October 3, 1854—School removed to Seventh street.

May 13, 1866—Supplementary act passed by the Legislature admitting pupils of the Society into the Boys' and Girls' High School.

    Legacy of Rosanna Osterman received.

October 28, 1867—Maimonides College opened with gratuitous services by Isaac Leeser, Marcus Jastrow, Sabato Morais and Aaron S. Bettelheim as instructors. Subsequently with similar services from Geo. Jacobs and Hyman Polano.

February 1, 1868—Isaac Leeser died.

1869—First regular annual contribution received from the Charity Ball Association.

1874—Legacies of Isaac Leeser and Jacob Bamberger received.

April 1, 1876—Twenty-fifth Anniversary of the Society's school celebrated at Concordia Hall, Callowhill near Fifth street.

March 3, 1878—School No. 2 opened in synagogue building of B'nai Israel, Fifth and Catharine streets.

September, 1878—English instruction temporarily discontinued in Society's school.

December 31, 1878—School No. 2 removed from Fifth and Catharine streets to 516 South street.

October 12, 1879—School No. 3 opened at Marshall street and Girard avenue.

December 28, 1879—Richmond School (No. 4) opened at 624 Wayne street.

December 31, 1879—School No. 2 removed to 417 Pine street.

1880—Abraham Adler (fifth President) died (during his incumbency).

January 26, 1880—School No. 3 removed to Fourth and Poplar streets.

September 1, 1880—Sewing school for girls opened in Richmond School.

March 13, 1881—Revised By-Laws adopted.

May 1, 1881—School No. 3 removed to 872 N. Seventh street.

June 6, 1881—School No. 1 temporarily removed to 872 N. Seventh street.

November 14, 1881—School re-opened at Seventh and Callowhill streets, and School No. 3 consolidated with it.

1882—Memorial fund of Abraham Adler received from Mrs. Adler.

September 16, 1883—2856-58 Lark street occupied by School No. 4, and industrial work for boys began in the building.

1883—Leeser Library catalogued by Cyrus Adler.

Legacy of Mayer Arnold received.

September 1, 1884—School No. 2 removed to Fifth and Gaskill streets.

June, 1886—Industrial School opened at Seventh and Callowhill streets.

Legacy of Mayer Gans received.

1886—Young Women's Union becomes branch of the Hebrew Education Society.

1887—Legacies of Abraham Sussman, Rachel Whitzstein and Rev. J. Frankel received.

April 17, 1888—School No. 2 removed to 316 S. Fourth street.

January 31, 1889—Sale of Seventh street school house ratified.

February, 1889—School No. 1 removed to 1204 Germantown avenue.

February 2, 1891—School No. 2 removed to 322 Bainbridge street.

March, 1891—English night school, trade school and Hebrew school opened at 322 Bainbridge street.

September 22, 1891—Corner stone of Touro Hall laid.

November 27, 1891—Dedication of Touro Hall.

December 14, 1891—School No. 2, night school and trade school removed to Touro Hall.

    Legacy of Bertha Gans received.

    Legacy of Ellen Phillips received.

September 1, 1892—First monthly allotment received from the Baron de Hirsch Fund.

1893—September and October—University Extension Lectures.

November, 1894 to January, 1895—University Extension Lectures.

    Legacies of David Hoffman and Leopold Furth received.

April 19, 1886—Young Women's Union formed an independent organization.

    Legacy of Solomon Gans received.

1896—First free synagogue service held in Touro Hall on Rosh Hashanna and Yom Kippur.

January, 1897—Rooms in Touro Hall granted to B'nai B'rith Manual Training School free of charge.

October, 1897—University Extension Lectures.

    Legacies of Simon Fleisher, Joseph Rosenbaum and Morris Sickels received.

January, 1898—University Extension Lectures.

    Free use of three rooms granted to Gratz College for its classes.

APPENDIX I.

FORMER SCHOOL HOUSE
SEVENTH STREET, BET. CALLOWHILL AND WOOD.

APPENDIX I.

HEBREW SCHOOLS.

School No. 1, Seventh and Wood Streets.

In January, 1878, a change was effected in the management of the School, only one teacher in Hebrew, Mr. Hyman Polano, and one teacher in English, Miss Charity S. Cohen, were retained for a time. The English branches were discontinued on June 28th of this year.

Mr. Polano also taught a class at the Foster Home, beginning January 1, 1878; this school was discontinued on January 16, 1879.

On January 1, 1881, Solomon Solis Cohen was appointed to the position of Hebrew teacher in place of Hyman Polano, who had resigned.

In January, 1881, a Fair was given by the Teachers' Association of the Hebrew Sunday-school, for the purpose of raising sufficient funds to repair the school house on Seventh street.

The Treasurer of the Hebrew Education Society, Mr. Simon B. Fleisher, received a check for $2,274.80 from Mr. Jacob Muhr, who acted as Treasurer of the Fair.

The building was renovated at a cost of five thousand dollars over and above the amount received from the Teachers' Association, for which amount a mortgage on the building was taken. One thousand dollars of this had been paid off previous to its sale to Messrs. Roig & Langsdorf.

The building was re-dedicated on November 13, 1881, just twenty-five years after the first dedication, which took place on November 12, 1856. Rev. S. Morais delivered the opening prayer and Rev. Dr. M. Jastrow delivered an address, the services were ended by the reading of the afternoon prayers by the Rev. S. Morais.

On Monday, June 6, 1881, this school was temporarily removed to 872 N. Seventh street.

The building at Seventh and Wood streets, having been altered and improved, was re-opened for school purposes on the 14th of November following.

On the first of June, 1882, this school and the one held at 872 N. Seventh street, were consolidated.

In April, 1887, the Trade School was opened, in which garment making and cutting, cigar making and carpentering were taught.

In February, 1889, this building having been sold, the Hebrew school was removed to 1204 Germantown avenue, where it is now located. On January 1, 1891, Miss Evelyn Bomeisler succeeded Henry S. Morais as teacher. She is the present incumbent.

SCHOOL NO. 2, FIFTH AND CATHARINE STREETS.

On Sunday, March 3, 1878, Hebrew School No. 2 was opened in the Synagogue Building (known as the Holland Schule), Fifth and Catharine streets, with Marcus E. Lam as the instructor.

On December 31st the school was removed to 516 South street, on December 31, 1879 to 417 Pine street, on September 1, 1884 it was removed to Dramatic Hall, Fifth and Gaskill streets; this building has since been altered and is now the Synagogue of the Congregation Emunath Israel Oheb Shalom.

On April 17, 1888, removed to 316 S. Fourth street, on February 2, 1891 to 322 Bainbridge street, and on December 14th of the same year the first session of the Hebrew school was held in Touro Hall, Tenth and Carpenter streets, where it is permanently located.

School No. 3, Girard Avenue and Marshall Street.

October 12, 1879, School No. 3 was opened at the N. W. cor. Marshall street and Girard avenue, with Cyrus Adler as the teacher.

On January 26, 1880, the school was removed to the N. E. cor. Fourth and Poplar streets. April 26, 1880, Henry S. Morais was chosen as teacher of this school, in place of Cyrus Adler, who took charge of that in Wayne street.

May 1, 1881, the school was removed to 872 N. Seventh street, whence it was subsequently merged with School No. 1 at Seventh and Callowhill streets.

School No. 4, 624 Wayne Street.

On December 28, 1879, a school was opened at 624 Wayne street, in the district of Richmond, with Dr. H. Max Gerstenkranz as instructor.

On April 26, 1880, Cyrus Adler was chosen as teacher for the Wayne street school.

On Sunday afternoon, September 16, 1883, the school house at 2656-58 Lark street was dedicated. In this building, in June, 1885, was undertaken the first instruction in various branches of trades by the Society.

Carpentering, cigar making, manufacturing picture-frames and dressmaking were taught.

On the 30th of December, 1883, Cyrus Adler resigned and was succeeded by Moses De Ford.

March 1, 1888, C. D. Spivak became teacher in Lark street school, he was succeeded in February, 1891, by George S. Seldes, who in turn was succeeded on September 1, 1892, by Isaac Husik. The latter resigned in December, 1898, and was succeeded by Hyman Grabosky, who remains in charge at the present time.

Sewing School.

The Sewing School at 624 Wayne street was opened in

SCHOOL HOUSE, 254 & 56 WEIGEL STREET, late St.

October, 1880, by Mrs. A. C. Van Beil, assisted by Mrs. Simeon H. Newhouse (who became its first Superintendent), Miss Simha C. Peixotto, Miss Mawson, Mrs. Joseph Herzog of New York, and D. Sulzberger of the Society.

Miss Rose Kauffman (Mrs. Moses Feustman) succeeded Mrs. Newhouse in December, 1881, and retained the position a short time and was succeeded by Mrs. Eva Coons at the opening of the school, October, 1882, who retained the position until 1888.

The report for the year ending March 3, 1884, was made by Miss Tinie Feustman (Mrs. Edward Goldstein), Acting Superintendent, owing to the absence of Mrs. Coons.

In the fall of 1888 Miss Hennie May (Mrs. Isaac Kahn) succeeded Mrs. Coons, and on the opening of the school, November 3, 1884, became Superintendent. The school having been opened by Mrs. Horace A. Nathans, who visited it each Sunday morning during that term.

Until this time the Sewing School had been conducted entirely by volunteer teachers and superintendents. The teachers in dress making and garment drafting were paid.

In the report for the year ending March 8, 1891, we note the following: "The Sewing School in Lark street is now conducted by two young girls who were former pupils, and who have been taught dress making and cutting in the garment drafting department, which has been in operation since last May (1890)."

It was found impracticable to continue the school in this manner, the children not having the proper respect for their teachers, who were unable to enforce discipline and who could not retain the attendance as did the ladies who formerly were the instructors; in consequence of this it was discontinued.

The following ladies were volunteer teachers during its existence.

SUPERINTENDENTS, ACTING SUPERINTENDENTS AND TEACHERS.

Mrs. Simeon H. Newhouse, Mrs. Eva Coons, Mrs. Horace

A. Nathans, Misses Celia Adler, Rose Kauffman, Tinie Feustman, Hennie May and Celia Hirshler; Misses Eckerson, Annie Jastrow, Minnie Rowe, Josephine Leberman, Leah Abeles, Salvena Shloss, Katinka Mansbach, Bertha Kohn, Ella Frank, Alice Kaufman, Bertha Guggenheimer, Fannie Allen, Florrie Shloss and Cora Hirshler.

General Night School.

March, 1891, a General Night School was opened at 322 Bainbridge street, with Bernard Harris and Amelia J. Allen as the teachers. It increased in size so rapidly that it soon required two additional teachers. This school was removed into the new building at Touro Hall on December 14, 1891, and is there permanently established under guidance of a corps of nine teachers. Besides the elementary branches of English there are here taught the following: To women and girls, dress making and millinery; to men and boys, cigar making, garment cutting, etc., and to both sexes, typewriting and stenography.

The teaching of various other industries and trades such as carpentering, tin working, upholstering, iron work, etc., had at different times been introduced in this school, but were necessarily abandoned by reason of a lack of adequate attendance.

LIST OF TEACHERS ENGAGED AT VARIOUS TIMES IN THE SCHOOLS OF THE HEBREW EDUCATION SOCIETY.

NIGHT SCHOOL.

Bernard Harris,
Augusta Selig,
Florence Kohn,
Jennie Charsken,
Corinne B. Arnold,
Ella Harris,
Mabel Lyons,
Gerson Levy,
Thomas Seltzer,
Samuel M. Israell.

Amelia J. Allen,
Evelyn Bomeisler,
Rosa Rosenstein,
Ida Casseras,
Mary Goldstein,
Kate Rosenstein,
Cecelia Sundheim,
Emma Brylawski,
Sarah Levin,
Edward Nathan.

SHORTHAND AND TYPEWRITING.

Eva Halpern, Rebecca Slobodkin.

KINDERGARTEN.

Diana Hirschler, Mary Goldstein,
Emma Brylawski.

NIGHT SCHOOL.—DRESSMAKING.

Mrs. Bloch,
Hannah Bachrach,
Celia Abrahams,
Sophia Benedick,
Theresa Reis,

Bella Blumenthal,
Bella Bachenheimer,
Gertrude Abrahams,
Jeanette Kauffman,
Etta Levy,

Mrs. A. J. Cortissoz.

MILLINERY.

Kate Gottlieb,
Tillie Wolfle.

Rosalie Hertzstein,
Florence R. Shill.

GARMENT CUTTING.

Adolph Lowenthal, Henry Armhold,
Max Stechert.

DRAWING.

Morris Sommers.

CARPENTERING.

H. Elsner, Jacob Gurwich,
Solomon Friedman, M. E. Arnold,
Henry Schwalm. J. Hindin.
Con. Brooks.

CIGAR MAKING.

H. Morris, —— Hart,
L. Hillersohn, Louis Friedman.
Abraham Koshland.

UPHOLSTERING.

Aaron Braunstein.

TINSMITHING.

B. Goldstein, John Bessmertney.

NIGHT SCHOOL—LARK STREET.

Samuel Deinard, A. J. Cortissoz.

HIGHER HEBREW—NIGHT SCHOOL.

Joseph Magil.

APPENDIX II.

APPENDIX II.

DONATIONS.

For the Year Ending March 25, 1879.

Jacob Loeb	$100	Isaac Rosskam	25
Lucien Moss	50	Levi Mayer	25
Mayer Sulzberger	50	Leon Berg	25
Moses A. Dropsie	50	Marks Brothers	25
Abraham Adler	50	Isaac Saller	10
Louis Gerstley	50	Henry Friedberger	10
Charles J. Cohen	50	Abraham Kahn	10
Aaron Lichten	50		
			$580

CONTRIBUTORS TO CATALOGUE FUND.

Reported March 10, 1883.

H. Friedberger	$10	S. Sternberger	10
Louis E. Levy	10	Henry Mitchell	5
Isaac Saller	10	George Wiener	5
Aaron Lichten	10		
M. C. Lichten	10		$150
D. Sulzberger	10		
Levi Mayer	10	All members of the Board of Officers, and from the Executors of the Leeser Estate	
Jacob Muhr	10		
Jacob Sulzberger	10		
Louis M. Frank	10	Hezekiah W. Arnold	10
Wm. Gerstley	10	Wm. B. Hackenburg	10
S. B. Fleisher	10	Mayer Sulzberger	10
Isaac Rosskam	10		$180

In the Treasurer's Report for the year ending March 9, 1884, we note the following contributions to the fund for the purchase of the Lark street building:

Rappaport Benevolent Association	$100 00	Isaac Rosskam	50 00
		Samuel Sternberger	50 00
Teachers' Association Hebrew Sunday School Society	100 00	Moses A. Dropsie	50 00
		Dr. E. Morwitz	50 00
		S. B. Fleisher	25 00
Isaac Saller	100 00	A. M. Frechie	25 00

Henry Gerstley	25 00	M. C. Lichten	10 00
Levi Mayer	25 00	Joseph Stern	10 00
Jacob Muhr	25 00	A. B. Kirschbaum	10 00
Philip Lewin	25 00	Jonas Langfeld	10 00
Simon Fleisher	25 00	Lazarus Mayer	10 00
Alexander Fleisher	25 00	Miss Ellen Phillips	10 00
Aaron Lichten	25 00	Mrs. Henry Cohen	10 00
Strouse, Loeb & Co.	25 00	Mrs. David H. Solis	10 00
M. Guggenheim	25 00	Mrs. Abraham S. Wolf	10 00
Mayer Sulzberger	25 00	Mrs. Eva Wolf	5 00
Loeb Brothers	25 00	Mrs. Isabella Louer	5 00
Louis Gerstley	25 00	Miss Isabel E. Cohen	5 00
A. E. Massman & Co.	25 00	Miss Blanche Teller	5 00
Leon Berg	25 00	Misses Guggenheimer	5 00
Mrs. M. Fleisher	25 00	M. Lazarus	5 00
Samuel Nathan	25 00	Jacob Miller	5 00
D'Israeli Literary Association		Henry M. Rosenbaum	5 00
tion	25 00	M. H. Lichten	5 00
Charles J. Cohen	25 00	Herman Weiller	5 00
Hirsh & Brother	25 00	I. M. Lang	5 00
From a fair given by Hattie Allman, Blanche Allman and Lydia Rains		Louis Pollock	5 00
		M. Bamberger	5 00
		Herman Heller	5 00
	22 76	H. S. Friedman	5 00
Abraham Kahn	20 00	Hanauer, Kohn & Co	5 00
Louis E. Levy	20 00	Henry S. Louchheim	5 00
Lucien Moss	20 00	Morris Newburger	5 00
Mayer Frank	10 00	Pfaelzer Bros. & Co.	5 00
George Wiener	10 00	Solomon Blumenthal	5 00
D. Sulzberger	10 00	H. S. Frank	5 00
A. M. Langfeld	10 00	Marks Goodman	5 00
B. Lowenstein	10 00	Henry L. Strouse	5 00
Charles Bloomingdale	10 00	Morris Dannenbaum	5 00
Henry Friedberger	10 00	Isidore Birgé	5 00
Louis Lang	10 00	Marcus Stern	5 00
Emanuel Schwerin	10 00	David Teller	5 00
Wm. B. Hackenburg	10 00	Joseph Herman Houtzdale	5 00
L. Rowe & Co	10 00		
B. W. Fleisher	10 00	Edwin Arnold	5 00
I. Kohn	10 00	Cash, K. B. & Co.	5 00
Louis M. Frank	10 00	Cash	5 00
M. M. Newman	10 00	Mrs. Simon Liveright	3 00
Jacob Sulzberger	10 00	A. Dannenbaum	2 00
M. H. Pulaski	10 00	Louis Wolf	2 00
William Gerstley	10 00	B. Kopf	2 00
S. & M. Liveright	10 00	Cash, S. & M.	1 00
Loeb & Schoenfelt	10 00		

$1462 76

SUBSCRIPTIONS TO INDUSTRIAL SCHOOL FUND.

March 8, 1885.

Moses A. Dropsie,	$50 00	Aug. B. Loeb,	10 00
Rosskam, Gerstley & Co	50 00	Leo Loeb	10 00
Samuel Sternberger	50 00	Louis Saller	10 00
Louis E. Levy	25 00	David M. Piza, N. Y.	10 00
Mrs. M. Fleisher, 2223 Green street	25 00	A. Lichten,	10 00
		Lazarus Mayer,	10 00
Isaac Saller	25 00	Alexander Fleisher,	10 00
S. B. Fleisher	25 00	Jeshurun Lodge, No. 59, I. O. B. B.	10 00
A. E. Massman, Pres. & Co.	25 00	Garrick Club,	10 00
M. Guggenheim	25 00	Penrose Fleisher,	10 00
Leon Berg,	25 00	George Wiener,	10 00
Lucien Moss,	25 00	Pfaelzer Bros. & Co.	10 00
Charles J. Cohen	25 00	Miss Ellen Phillips,	10 00
Mrs. Henry Cohen,	25 00	Miss Emily Phillips	10 00
Abr. Kahn,	25 00	M. M. Newman	10 00
Hirsh Brothers,	25 00	Female Hebrew Benevolent Society	10 00
Joseph Myers	25 00		
Nathan Strouse	20 00	Cash, F. M.	5 00
Mrs. Abr. S. Wolf	20 00	Mr. and Mrs. Mayer Louer	5 00
Isidore Coons,	20 00	Alexander Hexter,	5 00
Levi Mayer	15 00	Samuel Krieger	5 00
Joseph Rosenbaum,	15 00	Cash,	5 00
Philip Lewin,	15 00	Meyer Frank,	5 00
Simon Fleisher,	15 00	Col. L. May,	5 00
Ed. L. Rothschild	15 00	Miss Eleanor Samuels	5 00
Richmond Mission,	14 50	J. Bunford Samuels	5 00
Mrs. Amelia Hess, in memory of her husband,	12 50	Lavorno	5 00
		Wm. Moss, M. D.	5 00
		Mrs. E.	5 00
Simon Loeb	10 00	Miss Julia L. Moss,	5 00
D. Sulzberger	10 00	Miss Rebecca Moss,	5 00
Wolf & Co,	10 00	Sol. Rothschild,	5 00
Jonas Langfeld	10 00	John Samuels	5 00
Mr. and Mrs. I. Hyneman	10 00	Kohn, Adler & Co	5 00
Sol. Blumenthal	10 00	Miss Emily Phillips	5 00
Alfred C. Hirsh	10 00	Miss Ellen Phillips	5 00
Edward Loeb	10 00	Edward Lewin,	5 00
Max Liveright,	10 00	Mrs. David Elias,	5 00
Miss Louisa Gratz	10 00	H. F. Bachman	5 00
Miss Elizabeth Gratz	10 00	B. W. Fleisher,	5 00
Prof. Angelo Heilprin	10 00	Sarah Polack	5 00
Simon Liveright,	10 00	Miss Emily Solis,	5 00
Joshua Lodge, No. 23, I. O. B. B.	10 00	David H. Solis, Jr	5 00
		Dr. A. S. Isaacs, N. Y.	5 00

A. M. Langfeld	5 00	Henry Myers	5 00
M. H. Lichten	5 00	Myer Myers	5 00
H. S. Friedman	5 00	J. J. Hagedorn	5 00
H. M. Frank	5 00	H. Heller	5 00
Solomon Teller	5 00	Benj. F. Bloomingdale	5 00
David Teller	5 00	Sol. Thanhauser	3 00
Raphael Teller	5 00	Wm. Lichten	3 00
Jacob Wiener	5 00	Moses Espen	3 00
Abr. Wolf	5 00	Miss Ella Jacobs	2 00
B. F. Greenewald	5 00	Armand Dalsemer	2 00
Jacob Miller	5 00	Rev. N. Rosenau	2 00
Morris Liveright	5 00	Mrs. C. F. Bachman	2 00
A. M. Kohn	5 00	David Ettinger	2 00
S. Kohn	5 00	Mrs. Cornelia Kahn	2 00
L. L. & Co.	5 00	Raphael Green	2 00
Anton Iglauer	5 00	M. Roman	2 00
Herman Jonas	5 00	Sigmund Leerburger	1 00
Mr. Trieste, per Dr. Jastrow	5 00	Miss Rebecca Jacobs	1 00
		Mark Hassler	1 00
Mrs. Eva Wolf	5 00	Simon Hassler	1 00
Adolph Hyman	5 00	Miss Simha C. Peixotto	1 00
Myers & Appel	5 00	H. B. Sommer	1 00
Samuel Nathan	5 00	Mrs. H. J.	1 00
Mrs. Samuel Nathan	5 00	Miss Nina Morais	1 00
Morris Newburger	5 00		
			$1,250 00

DONATIONS.

March 14, 1886.

Isidore Coons	$200 00	Solomon Gans	25 00
Moses A. Dropsie	75 00	Mayer Sulzberger	25 00
Louis Gerstley	60 00	Hirsh Brothers	25 00
Mrs. Mayer Gans	50 00	M. Guggenheim	25 00
Samuel Sternberger	50 00	Miss Ellen Phillips	30 00
Isaac Rosskam	50 00	Miss Emily Phillips	20 00
M. Bamberger	25 00	Mrs. Henry Cohen	20 00
Rappaport Benevolent Association	25 00	Joseph Fels	17 38
		Philip Lewin	15 00
Marks Brothers	25 00	M. Fleisher	15 00
Nathan Strouse	25 00	B. W. Fleisher	10 00
Isaac Saller	25 00	Mrs. Abraham Adler	10 00
A. E. Massman	25 00	Levi Mayer	10 00
Simon B. Fleisher	25 00	Wolf & Co.	10 00
Abraham Kahn	25 00	Sulzberger & Co	10 00
Loeb Brothers	25 00	Andrew Kaas	10 00
H. Muhr's Sons	25 00	Henry Gerstley	10 00
Strouse, Loeb & Co.	25 00	William Gerstley	10 00

HEBREW EDUCATION SOCIETY.

Ed. L. Rothschild	10 00	Pen. Fleisher	5 00
Louis Eschner	10 00	L. N. Fleisher	5 00
Henry S. Frank	10 00	B. F. Greenewald	5 00
Mrs. Leon Berg	10 00	Alex. Fleisher	5 00
Louis E. Levy	10 00	S. Simon & Co.	5 00
Louis Saller	10 00	Morris Liveright	5 00
L. Bamberger	10 00	H. M. Frank	5 00
Marx B. Loeb	10 00	J. J. Hagedorn	5 00
Simon Loeb	10 00	H. S. Friedman	5 00
Wm. B. Hackenburg	10 00	Mayer Frank	5 00
M. W. Lipper	10 00	Isaac May	5 00
M. M. Newman	10 00	Bernard Selig	5 00
Max Liveright	10 00	Myers & Apple	5 00
Simon Liveright	10 00	Mrs. Eva Wolf	5 00
Female Hebrew Benevolent Society	10 00	Chas. Weinman	5 00
		Sol. L. Haas	5 00
Mrs. Abraham S. Wolf	10 00	Herman Heller	5 00
Lazarus Mayer	10 00	Wm. Jones	5 00
M. Dannenbaum	10 00	Sol. Blumenthal	5 00
Pfaelzer Brothers & Co	10 00	H. B. Blumenthal	5 00
Simon Fleisher	10 00	Samuel Hexter	5 00
Joseph Loeb	5 00	A. M. Langfeld	5 00
Dora Trieste	5 00	Rev. N. Rosenau	2 00
Leopold Hirsh	5 00		

DONATIONS TO INDUSTRIAL FUND.

March 13, 1887.

Isidore Coons	$100 00	S. Leopold & Brother	50 00
Strouse, Loeb & Co.	100 00	Joseph Netter & Co.	50 00
Snellenburg & Co	100 00	Moses A. Dropsie	50 00
Blumenthal Brothers & Co	100 00	Jacob Muhr	50 00
Liveright, Greenewald & Co.	100 00	S. Sternberger	25 00
		S. B. Fleisher	25 00
Fleisher Brothers	100 00	Louis Eschner	25 00
Frank Brothers & Co.	100 00	Isaac Saller	25 00
Miss Ellen Phillips	100 00	Philip Lewin	25 00
Miss Emily Phillips	100 00	Ed. L. Rothschild	25 00
Levi Mayer	55 00	Marks Brothers	25 00
Isaac Rosskam	50 00	Solomon Gans	25 00
Joseph Goldsmith & Co	50 00	Aaron Lichten	25 00
Hexter Brothers	50 00	Joseph Fels	25 00
Goldstein, Friedman & Co	50 00	Richmond Ind'r'l School	25 00
Goodman Brothers	50 00	Chas. Klein & Co.	25 00
A. Bachrach & Co	50 00	Lisberger & Wise	25 00
A. B. Kirschbaum & Co	50 00	D. Meyers & Co	25 00
Kohn, Rosenheim & Co.	50 00	Schloss & Loeb	25 00

154 HEBREW EDUCATION SOCIETY.

Louis E. Levy,	25 00	August B. Loeb	10 00
Stoneman Brothers	25 00	Edward Loeb	10 00
Joseph Louchheim,	25 00	Louis Saller	10 00
Mrs. Meyer Gans,	25 00	Andrew Kaas	10 00
Mayer Sulzberger	25 00	Mrs. Leon Berg	10 00
Mrs. H. A. Nathans	25 00	Mrs. A. S. Wolf	10 00
Espen Brothers	25 00	Lazarus Mayer,	10 00
M. Guggenheim	25 00	B. W. Fleisher,	10 00
Hirsh & Brothers	25 00	Mark Schwartz	10 00
Herman Heller	20 00	A. E. Massman	10 00
L. Bamberger & Co.	20 00	A. Hexter	5 00
Mrs. Henry Cohen,	20 00	David Teller	5 00
Grace Aguilar Sewing		Leopold Hirsh.	5 00
School,	15 00	Solomon Teller,	5 00
Moyer Fleisher,	15 00	David Solis Cohen	5 00
Grace Aguilar Lit. Society	14 00	Proceeds of Fair	3 00
Pfaelzer Brothers & Co,	10 00	Sarah Lavenson	1 80

DONATIONS TO INDUSTRIAL FUND.

March 11, 1888.

Miss Ellen Phillips	$100 00	Espen Brothers	25 00
Miss Emily Phillips	50 00	Max Bamberger	25 00
Isaac Bosskam,	75 00	M. Guggenheim	25 00
Isidore Coons	50 00	Hirsh & Brother,	25 00
Moses A. Dropsie	50 00	Mrs. Bertha Gans	25 00
Jacob Muhr	50 00	Fleisher Brothers	25 00
Philip Lewin,	25 00	Mrs. Abraham S. Wolf,	20 00
Liveright, Greenewald & Co.	25 00	Mrs. Dora Trieste (in memory of her son, Sidney)	20 00
N. Snellenburg & Co.,	25 00		
Louis Gerstley,	25 00	Louis Saller	15 00
Samuel Sternberger	25 00	Moyer Fleisher,	15 00
Morris Newburger,	25 00	Simon Loeb	10 00
Nathan Strouse	25 00	Louis Reinheimer	10 00
Strouse, Loeb & Co,	25 00	Lissburger & Wise	10 00
Isaac Saller	25 00	S. Wilson & Son	10 00
Louis Eschner	25 00	Meyer Seidenbach	10 00
Joseph Fels	25 00	Wm. B. Hackenburg	10 00
Simon Fleisher,	25 00	Edward Loeb	10 00
Hanauer, Kohn & Co.,	25 00	Pfaelzer Brothers & Co.	10 00
Simon B. Fleisher	25 00	Mrs. Leon Berg	10 00
Aaron Lichten,	25 00	Andrew Kaas	10 00
Marks Brothers	25 00	B. W. Fleisher,	10 00
L. Bamberger	25 00	Frank Brothers & Co.	10 00
Solomon Gans	25 00	Aaron Gans	10 00
Mayer Sulzberger	25 00	Jacob Miller & Son,	10 00

A. B. Kirschbaum	10 00	Samuel Fishleder	5 00
Levi Mayer	10 00	Stoneman Brothers & Co.	5 00
D. Bacharach	5 00	Joseph Netter & Co	5 00
D. Myers	5 00	Chas. Stein	5 00
Julius Loeb	5 00	Eugene Loeb	5 00
S. Teller	5 00	Joseph A. Louchheim	5 00
H. Heller	5 00	Cash	5 00
Hirsh, Frank & Co.	5 00	Cora Hushier	3 00
Charles Meyers	5 00	Sarah Lavenson	
Daniel Meyers	5 00	M. Goldsmith	2 00
H. B. Blumenthal	5 00	Philip Fleisher	2 00
Sol. Blumenthal	5 00	S. Lehman	2 00
A. M. Langfeld	5 00	I. C. Levi	1 00
Augustus B. Reger	5 00	B. Baruch	1 00
B. Selig	5 00	Alfred A. Marcus, one dozen Daily Prayer Books	
Henry M. Reis	5 00		
Sol. L. Haas	5 00	Jos. Fels, Box Laundry Soap	
Henry M. Frank	5 00		
Daniel Myers, Jr	5 00	Anonymous, Norman and Courtney prizes	10 00
Chas. Goodman	5 00		

DONATIONS TO INDUSTRIAL FUND.

March 10, 1889.

Miss Ellen Phillips	$100 00	Hanauer, Kohn & Co	25 00
Miss Emily Phillips, $75		Liveright, Greenewald & Co.	25 00
Prize in Carpenter Shop	95 00	Morris Newburger & Sons	25 00
	20	Espen Brothers	25 00
Isaac Rosskam	50 00	Hirsh & Brother	25 00
Isidor Coons	50 00	Leopold Bamberger	25 00
Moses A. Dropsie	50 00	Max Bamberger	25 00
H. Muhr's Sons	50 00	M. Guggenheim	25 00
Joseph Fels	25 00	Mrs. Bertha Gans	25 00
H. Gerstley	25 00	N. Snellenburg & Co.	25 00
Louis Eschner	25 00	Penrose Fleisher	15 00
Isaac Salter	25 00	Jacob Miller & Sons	15 00
Philip Lewin	25 00	Through Miss Esther Baum for the Industrial Schools from the following little girls: Gertie Reis, Hilda Blumenthal, Carrie Simon, Addie Stern, Rena Wolf, Selma Blumenthal, Hortense Wolf and Blanche Schwartz	11 50
Louis E. Levy	25 00		
Marks Brothers	25 00		
Moyer Fleisher	25 00		
Simon B. Fleisher	25 00		
Mayer Sulzberger	25 00		
Samuel Sternberger	25 00		
Nathan Strouse	25 00		
Strouse, Loeb & Co	25 00		
Solomon Gans	25 00		
Simon Fleisher	25 00	B. Lob	10 00

Daniel Meyers, Jr.	10 00	Jos. C. Greenewald.	5 00
H. S. Frank.	10 00	Charles Shoneman.	5 00
Sol. L. Haas	10 00	A. Hexter	5 00
M. Frank	10 00	Dan. Meyers.	5 00
Hexter Brothers	10 00	Jos. Koch	5 00
Loeb & Louchheim	10 00	S. Fishleder	5 00
M. B. Loeb	10 00	J. S. Frank	5 00
August B. Loeb	10 00	Klein, Putzel & Co.	5 00
W. B. Hackenburg	10 00	Leopold Hirsh	5 00
Pfaelzer Brothers & Co.	10 00	David Klein	5 00
Blum Brothers.	10 00	L. Reinheimer.	5 00
B. W. Fleisher.	10 00	Isaac M. Lang	5 60
Andrew Kaas	10 00	H. Weiller.	5 00
Mrs. Abr. S. Wolf.	10 00	Herman Heller.	5 00
Lucien Moss.	10 00	Simon Loeb.	5 00
H. B. Blumenthal.	5 00	Goldsmith & Co	2 00
D. Myers	5 00	Cash.	2 00
Henry M. Reis.	5 00	Cash.	2 00
B. Selig	5 00		

SUBSCRIPTIONS TO BUILDING FUND, TOURO HALL.

S. W. COR. TENTH AND CARPENTER STREETS.

MARCH 13, 1892.

Moses A. Dropsie.	$1,500 00	Mason Hirsh.	250 00
Miss Ellen Phillips.	1,000 00	Henry Hirsh.	250 00
Jacob Muhr.	1,000 00	Simon B. Fleisher.	250 00
Moyer Fleisher.	750 00	Andrew Kaas	250 00
Isaac Rosskam.	500 00	Mayer Sulzberger	250 00
Louis Eschner.	500 00	Sam'l Snellenburg.	250 00
Simon Fleisher.	500 00	Wm. B. Hackenburg.	200 00
Louis Gerstley	500 00	Mr. and Mrs. Simon Pfaelzer.	200 00
Kohn, Adler & Co.	500 00	Mrs. H. A. Nathans.	200 00
Sam'l Sternberger.	500 00	Aaron Lichten	200 00
Marks Brothers.	500 00	Hagedorn & Merz.	200 00
Young Women's Union.	500 00	Mr. and Mrs. Max Bamberger.	200 00
Solomon Gans	500 00		
Elias Wolf & Sons.	300 00	Morris Dannenbaum.	200 00
Levi Mayer	250 00	Espen Brothers	200 00
Isaac Saller	250 00	Jos. Louchheim	200 00
Isidor Coons.	250 00	Wolf & Co.	200 00
Wm. Gerstley	250 00	Jos. J. Snellenburg.	200 00
Morris Pfaelzer	250 00	Philip Lewin	150 00
Penrose Fleisher.	250 00	Mr. and Mrs. Simon Liveright.	150 00
Joseph Rosenbaum.	250 00		
Benj. W. Fleisher.	250 00	Joseph Fels.	100 00
Mrs. Bertha Gans.	250 00		

HEBREW EDUCATION SOCIETY. 157

D. Sulzberger	100 00	Cash. Dr. M.	100 00
Louis E. Levy	100 00	Phiz Muhr.	100 00
Simon Loeb	100 00	Henry M. Reis.	100 00
Louis Saller	100 00	Raphael Teller.	100 00
Henry Gerstley	100 00	Sol. Blumenthal	100 00
David Teller	100 00	Stern & Brothers.	100 00
Mrs. Abraham S. Wolf.	100 00	Herman Jonas	100 00
Horace Moses	100 00	Nathan Klein	100 00
Emil Cauffman	100 00	W. S. & M. Lieber	100 00
Mrs. H. Dannenbaum	100 00	Jos. R. Teller	100 00
H. A. Jeitles	100 00	M. Powdermaker	100 00
Samuel S. Fels.	100 00	Samuel Hexter.	100 00
Solomon Teller.	100 00	Leo Loeb.	100 00
Leopold Hirsh.	100 00	Daniel Strouse.	100 00
Emanuel Springer	100 00	Nathan Strouse	100 00
James M. Jeitles.	100 00	Isidor Sultzbach	100 00
Henry Rothschild	100 00	Mrs. M. Friedenwald.	100 00
H. B. Blumenthal	100 00	S. K. Louchheim.	
Mrs. Levi Strouse	100 00	W. C. Louchheim,	
Adam Gimbel	100 00	J. H. Louchheim,	100 00
Karl Straus	100 00	At Silver Wedding	
Alfred C. Hirsh	100 00	of Parents,	
Mrs. Z. L. Eisner.	100 00	S. L. Bloch	100 00
Mrs. A. E. Massman.	100 00	Morris Liveright	75 00
A. M. Frechie	100 00	Mrs. Alex Fleisher	75 00
I. Herzberg	100 00	Leopold Loeb & Co.	75 00
B. Labe & Son.	100 00	David Hoffman	50 00
Leopold Bamberger	100 00	Wm. Lichten & Co.	50 00
Jacob Miller Sons & Co.	100 00	J. S. Rosengarten	50 00
Mrs. Minnie K. Arnold	100 00	Landauer & Strauss	50 00
Mrs. Jacob Loeb	100 00	Mrs. B. P. Wedelle.	50 00
Walter S. Berg.	100 00	Eli Wineland	50 00
I. Behal & Sons	100 00	Mayer, Son & Co.	50 00
Isaac Blum.	100 00	Mrs. Leon Berg, New York.	50 00
Gabriel Blum.	100 00	Chas. Weinman & Co	50 00
Ralph Blum	100 00	Chas. Shoneman	50 00
Max Liveright.	100 00	Louis Shoneman	50 00
Louis Fleisher	100 00	Edwin Arnold	50 00
Mrs. Moses Nathans	100 00	H. M. Frank.	50 00
Marx B. Loeb.	100 00	E. Benswanger.	50 00
Mrs. Henry S. Frank	100 00	Master Albert Arnold	50 00
Mayer Frank.	100 00	S. Zweighaft.	50 00
Mrs. Abr. Adler	100 00	Jacob Wiener	50 00
Mayer Seidenbach	100 00	A. Bacharach	50 00
Theresa Seidenbach	100 00	Zineman & Brothers	50 00
Henry Seidenbach.	100 00	H. S. Friedman	50 00
Joseph Koch.	100 00	Simon Abeles	50 00
Simon Kohn.	100 00	B. Lowenstein.	50 00

Kayser & Allman	50 00	Jos. Marschuetz	25 00
Greenewald & Co	50 00	Dr. L. W. Steinbach	25 00
E. Silberstein	50 00	Joseph Loeb	25 00
Chas. H. Vendig	50 00	Herman Weiller	25 00
Marc Sternberg	50 00	Strouse, Rothschild & Co.	25 00
Solomon Asher	50 00	Miss Mathilda Kahn	25 00
J. M. Engel	50 00	Miss Fredora Kahn	25 00
Morris May	50 00	L. H. Vendig	25 00
H. S. Louchheim	50 00	Julius Sondheim	25 00
Chas. Elias	50 00	Morris Rosenberg	25 00
Henry L. Strouse	50 00	A. I. Uffenheimer	25 00
L. Bachenheimer	50 00	S. Bacharach	25 00
Jacob Tuck	50 00	Alkus Brothers & Co.	25 00
Mark Schwartz	50 00	Rev. Dr. H. Illowizi	25 00
David Stern, New York	50 00	Ignatz Klein	25 00
Adam Baum & Son	50 00	M. Rosenbaum	25 00
Rev. Dr. Jos. Krauskopf	50 00	Mayer Strouse	25 00
Benj. Mayer	50 00	Joseph Loeb	25 00
H. M. Rosenbaum	50 00	John Netter	25 00
Chas. Goodman	50 00	Dr. Morris Jastrow, Jr.	25 00
Solomon Miller	50 00	Furth & Singer	25 00
Isaac H. Kahn	50 00	B. Abeles	25 00
Frank Teller	50 00	Jos. E. Sulzberger	25 00
Lewis Rowe	50 00	I. Steppacher	25 00
Ludwig M. Leberman	50 00	B. F. Greenwald	25 00
A. Herzberg	50 00	B. Selig	25 00
S. Kirschbaum	50 00	Morris Jaretzky	25 00
D. Kirschbaum	50 00	Sylvan Dalsimer	25 00
Abe Hirsh	50 00	Jacob Henly	25 00
D. Hirsh	50 00	M. A. Kauffman	25 00
Samuel Kind	50 00	Sol. Selig	25 00
S. Leopold & Sons	40 00	Joseph Myers	25 00
Jacob S. Frank	25 00	Charles J. Cohen	25 00
Jacob Stern	25 00	Louis Teller	25 00
Friedoline Mayer	25 00	Chas. Techner	25 00
Mrs. Mina May	25 00	Simon A. Stern	25 00
Mrs. Louis Walker	25 00	Louis Hano	25 00
W. M. Steppacher	25 00	August Wise	25 00
Mrs. Elvira N. Solis	25 00	Joseph Dreifus	25 00
Miss Amelia Mayer	25 00	Jacob Schwartz & Co.	25 00
David H. Solis	25 00	Hart Blumenthal	25 00
Daniel Myers	25 00	Mark Simons	25 00
L. Rosenberg	25 00	Bernard Kirschbaum	25 00
Ostheimer Brothers	25 00	J. E. Hyneman	25 00
C. O. Nathans	25 00	Arnold Kohn	25 00
A. Reinheimer	25 00	Abraham M. Kohn	25 00
Samuel Cohen	25 00	Moses H. Wiener	25 00
Krieger Brothers	25 00	Adolph Rosenbaum	25 00

HEBREW EDUCATION SOCIETY. 159

Jacob Rothschild, Cawker City, Kan.	25 00
Samuel Hecht	22 50
Rev. Dr. S. Morais	20 00
Rev. Dr. M. Jastrow	20 00
Mark Katz	20 00
Fred'k Wertheimer	20 00
Zellner Brothers	20 00
George Spiro	20 00
Jacob Cartun	20 00
Ed. Ziegler	20 00
Mayer L. Kahn	20 00
Edwin Lewin	20 00
Wm. Morris	20 00
Rev. S. Kaufman	20 00
A. Rabinowitz & Co.	15 00
Herman Kraus	15 00
Jacob Moscowitz	15 00
S. White	15 00
S. Sternberger	15 00
Kohn & Kline	15 00
B. Newman	15 00
A. Ellis	15 00
H. Berkowitz	15 00
L. Wollenberger	15 00
Kiva Schwartz	15 00
E. Lederer	15 00
Oscar B. Teller	15 00
Chas. Gilles	15 00
Children of First Class Hebrew School, Congregation Adath Jeshurun	11 36
Isaac Hamburg	10 00
Abe Strouse	10 00
H. B. Sommer	10 00
Chas. K. Stern	10 00
Moses H. Stern	10 00
I. Katzenberg	10 00
A. Gluckman	10 00
A. H. Marcus	10 00
Jacob Jacobson	10 00
Master Sol. M. Myerhoff	10 00
M. Pomeranz	10 00
M. Ostrow & Son	1 00
David Nathans	1 00
M. Goldberg	1 00
Samuel Berkowitz	1 00
S. Weiss	1 00
J. N. Israel	10 00
Mrs. Nina Morais Cohen, in memory of Julia Eckstein	10 00
Joseph Adler	10 00
W. Stern	10 00
Gutman Kline	10 00
Emil Meyerhoff	10 00
David Markowitz	10 00
S. Rothschild	10 00
Martin Frank	10 00
Adolph Newman	10 00
Dr. A. B. Hirsh	10 00
Simon Miller	10 00
Wm. Goldberger	10 00
Abraham Katz	10 00
Sigmund Marks	10 00
H. Milder	10 00
Raphael S. Green	10 00
Children's Fair:	
Ida Hess, Hulda Lewin, Essie Hassler, Carrie Kahn, Minnie Goldsmith	9 32
Bertha and Minnie Miller, Pottstown	8 00
W. Gerson	5 00
Mrs. Jenny Kessler	5 00
Wm. West	5 00
Halpron Brothers	5 00
P. H. Strausman	5 00
Louis Stein	5 00
A. Zeussler	5 00
D. Rosezweig	5 00
M. Goodfriend	5 00
Misses Jacobs	5 00
Abr. Silverman	5 00
Morris Weiss	5 00
Samuel Pullitzer	5 00
P. Greenberg	5 00
L. Schlager	5 00
Miss Charity Solis Cohen	5 00
S. Rosenthal	5 00
Jos. Wehman	5 00
L. Siegel	5 00
Mrs. Mary Hart	5 00
M. Sarginsky	5 00
A. Pomeranz	5 00
S. Solms	5 00

HEBREW EDUCATION SOCIETY.

M. Silberman	5 00	Rev. S. M. Fleischman	5 00
Ellis & Brown	5 00	Sol. Grunwalt	5 00
D. Miller	5 00	Max Roth	5 00
L. Applebaum	5 00	D. Markowitz	5 00
I. Newrock	5 00	David Sacks	5 00
Henry Wirtshafter	5 00	F. Teitelbaum	5 00
Isaac Greenstone	5 00	H. Kris	5 00
Max Weiss	5 00	H. Wolf	5 00
Henry Weiss	5 00	Jacob Behrend	5 00
H. Rosenthal	5 00	L. Schlesinger	5 00
Frank Wirtshafter	5 00	Chas. M. Lam	5 00
Leopold Kline	5 00	A. Newman	5 00
Isaac Weiss	5 00	R. Reichert	5 00
M. Hirschman	5 00	D. Rosenthal	5 00
Julius Kuttner	5 00	Mrs. Sarah Gans	5 00
Louis Lewin	5 00	Mrs. D. Pottsdamer	4 00
M. Lowenthal	5 00	Gratz Mordecai	4 00
Gustav Lipschmetz	5 00	Percy A. Sanguinetti	4 00
Jacob Miller	5 00	Fabian Kline	2 00
S. L. Mendel	5 00	Anonymous	2 00

RECEIVED FROM THE HEBREW SUNDAY-SCHOOL SOCIETY FOR BUILDING FUND.

Subscriptions obtained by the pupils	$568 35	Mr. S. Baker	10 00
Mrs. Minnie K. Arnold	110 00	Nathan Strouse	10 00
Miss Ellen Phillips	100 00	Benj Schloss	10 00
Mrs. A. S. Wolf	100 00	David Stern	10 00
Sol. Gans (in memory of his wife)	100 00	Eph. Lederer	10 00
		B. F. Greenewald	10 00
Lazarus Mayer	100 00	Miss F. Goldstein	10 00
Mrs. Emil Cauffman	100 00	Mrs. H. Hahn	10 00
M. Lieber (proceeds of Raffle)	57 00	Mrs. S. Liveright	10 00
		Cash	5 00
Philadelphia Sewing Society	48 50	Allen H. Muhr, W. P. Muhr	5 00
		Mrs. H. Simpson	5 00
Mrs. Bertha Gans	30 00	H. B. Sommer	5 00
B. W. Fleisher	25 00	Miss Ida H. Casseres	5 00
Moses A. Dropsie	25 00	Mrs. I. Casseres	5 00
Mrs. Leon Berg	25 00	Chas. H. Vendig	5 00
Alfred Myers	25 00	Mrs. Chas. H. Vendig	5 00
H. S. Friedman	20 00	S. Weil	5 00
Mrs. Sarah Polock	20 00	Wm. Lichten	5 00
Mrs. S. Newhouse	20 00	A. H. Marcus	5 00
Miss Julia Moss	12 50	A Friend	5 00
Miss Josephine Moss		Mrs. M. Oppenheimer	5 00

Chas. M. Lam	2 00	J. Auerbach—pupils	(6)
Abr. S. W. Rosenbach	1 00	Interest on above	171 90
J. S. Dreifuss	1 00		
Miss Sternberg	50	Total	$1,815 81

Furniture Fund.

Benj. F. Teller	$150 00	Aaron Lichten	25 00
Moses A. Dropsie	100 00	Herman Jonas	25 00
Moyer Fleisher	100 00	Henry Gerstley	25 00
Louis Gerstley	100 00	Isaac Kohn	25 00
Cash S. M.	100 00	Samuel Kohn	25 00
Wolf & Co.	100 00	Morris Pfaelzer	25 00
Mrs. Wm. B. Hackenburg	100 00	Henry Rothschild	25 00
Simon Fleisher	50 00	Mayer Frank	25 00
Mrs. H. A. Nathans	50 00	Leopold Loeb & Co.	25 00
Isaac Rosskam	50 00	Marks Brothers	25 00
Ed. Loeb	50 00	Joseph Koch	25 00
Mrs. I. Sultzbach	50 00	Isaac Mansbach	25 00
H. B. Blumenthal	50 00	Morris Einstein	25 00
Benj. Labe & Son	50 00	Simon May	25 00
Henry M. Reis	50 00	Espen Brothers	25 00
M. W. Lipper	50 00	Mrs. H. S. Frank	25 00
Wm. Gerstley	50 00	B. W. Fleisher	25 00
Simon Liveright	50 00	Aaron Lichten	25 00
Isaac Saller	25 00	Aaron Gans	25 00
Dr. Morris Jastrow	25 00	S. B. Fleisher	25 00
Philip Lewin	25 00	August B. Loeb	25 00
Louis Saller	25 00	Joseph Fels	25 00
A. M. Frechie	25 00	B. Selig	25 00
Mrs. Abr. S. Wolf	25 00	Blum Brothers	25 00
Mrs. S. Espen	25 00	Simon Loeb	10 00
Strouse, Loeb & Co.	25 00	Jacob Miller Sons & Co.	10 00
M. Sulzberger	25 00	H. M. Rosenbaum	10 00
S. Nirdlinger	25 00	Raphael Teller	10 00
Wolf Brothers	25 00	Solomon Teller	10 00
Miss Emily Phillips	25 00	Angelo Hirsch	10 00
Sam. Sternberger	25 00	Cash (J. K.)	10 00
Max Bamberger	25 00	Morris Liveright	10 00
Leopold Bamberger	25 00	B. F. Greenewald	10 00
Cash J. M.	25 00	Adam Baum & Co.	10 00
Andrew Kaas	25 00	Morris Dannenbaum	10 00
Penrose Fleisher	25 00	Louis Fleisher	10 00
Max Liveright	25 00	Abe Hirsh	10 00
Sol. L. Haas	25 00	Leopold Hirsh	10 00
Louis Teller	25 00	E. Wineland	10 00
Joseph Loeb	25 00	H. J. Tickner	10 00
Jacob Stern & Sons	25 00	Julius Siehel	10 00

Sol. Miller	10 00	Morris Lang, 45 North	
Samuel Greenewald	10 00	Third Street	5 00
Miss Ella Jacobs	5 00	Alex. M. Apple	5 00
N. L. Mayer	5 00	Jos. Goldsmith	5 00
Mark Katz	5 00	David H. Solis	5 00
Will Stern	5 00	Ed. Arnold	5 00
S. Rothschild	5 00		

BUILDING FUND ACCOUNT.

Cash from old building, Seventh and Wood Streets	$7,957 61
Interest on this amount	128 44
Subscription to Building Fund paid in	29,863 04
Interest	78 90
Furniture Fund	2,655 00
Mortgage	15,000 00
	$55,682 99
Amount paid out	51,576 06
Balance	4,106 93
Less special deposit for Janitor's Lodge	616 05
	$3,490 88

FROM THE ANNUAL REPORT.

MARCH 10, 1895.

SUBSCRIPTIONS TO FUND FOR PURCHASING A PIANO.

Messrs. James Bellak's Sons	$75 00	L. Katzenberg	5 00
		Louis Gerstley	5 00
Young Men's Hebrew Association	28 00	Isaac Rosskam	5 00
		Jacob Muhr	5 00
Miss Emily Phillips	10 00	Edward Wolf	5 00
Mrs. Andrew Kaas	5 00	Louis Eschner	5 00
Mrs. Eva Coons	5 00	Levi Mastbaum	5 00
Mrs. M. Friedenwald	5 00	Benj. Wolf	5 00
Gabriel Blum	5 00	Moyer Fleisher	5 00
Mrs. Horace A. Nathans	8 00	Mrs. H. S. Louchheim	2 00
D. Sulzberger	5 00	Cash	2 00
Lucien Moss	5 00	Total	$200 00

RECEIPTS FROM HEBREW CHARITY BALLS.

1861	$ 75 00	1883	600 00
1862	75 00	1884	600 00
1869	400 00	1885	600 00
1870	454 80	1886	600 00
1871	917 77	1887	600 00
1872	1,029 83	1888	600 00
1873	1,188 12	1889	600 00
1874	1,128 34	1890	600 00
1875	1,298 41	1891	800 00
1876	1,273 26	1892	924 85
1877	1,180 33	1893	900 00
1878	600 00	1894	700 00
1879	200 00	1895	700 00
1880	500 00	1896	550 00
1881	500 00	1897	422 71
1882	600 00	1898	500 00

FIFTY-FIRST ANNUAL REPORT

OF THE

Hebrew Education Society

OF

Philadelphia.

For the Year Ending March 1,

1899.

Executive Officers.

President . . . . BENJAMIN WOLF
Vice-President . . . . . EPHRAIM LEDERER
Treasurer . . . . GABRIEL BLUM
Honorary Secretary . . DAVID SULZBERGER

HONORARY LIFE MEMBERS OF THE BOARD OF OFFICERS.

MOSES A. DROPSIE,   ISAAC ROSSKAM.

Board of Officers.

Term expires 1906.
LOUIS E. LEVY,
MRS. HORACE A. NATHANS,
MRS. HENRY S. LOUCHHEIM,
SAMUEL M. HYNEMAN,
DAVID W. AMRAM.

Term expires 1904.
LOUIS GERSTLEY,
JACOB MUHR,
EDWARD WOLF,
MRS. FLORENCE K. LIVERIGHT,
WM. B. ROSSKAM.

Term expires 1905.
ANDREW KAAS,
MRS. EVA COONS,
HENRY M. FRANK,
MAURICE BAMBERGER,
BENJ. W. FLEISHER, JR.

Librarian   REBECCA SLOBODKIN.

Standing Committees 1899.

EXECUTIVE AND FINANCE.

Gabriel Blum,
Benjamin Wolf,
Louis Gerstley,
Edward Wolf,
Ephraim Lederer.

BUILDING, PROPERTY AND SUPPLIES.

D. Sulzberger,
B. W. Fleisher, Jr.,
Andrew Kaas,
Mrs. Horace A. Nathans,
Mrs. Florence K. Liveright.

INDUSTRIAL—MEN'S.

Henry M. Frank,
Maurice Bamberger,
Jacob Muhr,
Louis Gerstley,
Wm. B. Rosskam.

INDUSTRIAL—WOMEN'S.

Mrs. H. A. Nathans,
Mrs. H. S. Louchheim,
Mrs. Florence K. Liveright,
Mrs. Eva Coons.

MEMBERSHIP.

Edward Wolf,
Mrs. H. S. Louchheim,
Maurice Bamberger,
Henry M. Frank,
Andrew Kaas,
Wm. B. Rosskam,
Benj. W. Fleisher, Jr.

READING ROOM AND LIBRARY.

Samuel M. Hyneman,
D. W. Amram,
Louis E. Levy,
Mrs. Eva Coons,
Jacob Muhr.

EDUCATION.

Louis E. Levy,
Samuel M. Hyneman,
B. W. Fleisher, Jr.,
D. W. Amram,
Mrs. Eva Coons.

LEESER LIBRARY.

D. Sulzberger,
D. W. Amram,
Samuel M. Hyneman.

Fifty-First Annual Meeting.

PHILADELPHIA, March 12, 1899.

The Fifty-First Annual Meeting of the Hebrew Education Society was held this morning in Touro Hall, S. W. corner of Tenth and Carpenter streets. Ephraim Lederer, Vice President in the chair and D. Sulzberger acting as Secretary.

The minutes of the last meeting were read and approved.

The reports of the President and Treasurer were received and read, and ordered to be entered on the minutes.

On motion of Mr. Edward Wolf, seconded by Mr. Louis Gerstley, it was carried that one thousand copies of the Annual Report be printed for distribution, together with the history of the Society.

A communication was received from Messrs. Baker & Dallett, architects, in reference to the alterations and repairs in Touro Hall.

On motion of Mr. Louis E. Levy, seconded by Mr. Samuel M. Hyneman, it was carried that the report be received and filed.

Nominations now being in order, the present incumbents, whose terms expired, were all renominated as follows:

FOR ONE YEAR.

President—Benjamin Wolf.
Vice-President—Ephraim Lederer.
Treasurer—Gabriel Blum.
Secretary—D. Sulzberger.

BOARD OF OFFICERS FOR THREE YEARS.

Andrew Kaas.   Mrs. Eva Coons.
Henry M. Frank,   Maurice Bamberger.
            Benjamin W. Fleisher, Jr.

There being but one nominee for each position, on motion it was carried that the Secretary cast the vote of the Society, the nominees were declared unanimously elected.

On motion of Mr. Kaas, seconded by Mr. Levy, it was carried that the communication from the architects, Messrs. Baker & Dallett, in reference to alterations and repairs and the removal of the swimming pool for which twelve additional shower-baths should be erected, should be taken up for consideration.

On motion of Mr. Edward Wolf, seconded by Mr. Gerstley, it was carried that the matter be referred to the Board of Officers with power to act.

On motion of Mr. Louis Gerstley, seconded by Mr. Edward Wolf, it was carried that the Committee on Membership be requested to use all possible efforts to enlarge the list of members, and a request was made that the names of the Committee on Membership be read; they are as follows: Edward Wolf, chairman, Mrs. H. S. Louchheim, Maurice Bamberger, Henry M. Frank, Andrew Kaas, William B. Rosskam and Benjamin W. Fleisher, Jr.

The Chairman stated that the same Committee would be continued for the coming year.

On motion adjourned.

D. SULZBERGER,
Secretary.

Fifty-First Annual Report.

To the Members, Patrons, Friends and Contributors of the Hebrew Education Society:

Ladies and Gentlemen.—

I regret that this, my first report as President of your Society, must be submitted in my absence; only the most urgent business requirements could have prevented my attendance at the Annual Meeting, more especially since only a portion of the amount required for the liquidation of the Nine Thousand Dollar mortgage has been subscribed.

The Society's history will be published this year with the regular Annual Report, and will prove a valuable acquisition to the history of the Jews in Philadelphia.

I trust that when the public shall receive this report, the entire subscription for the payment of the mortgage will have been obtained.

HEBREW SCHOOLS.

The examinations of the Hebrew Schools were held as follows:

No. 1, June 3, 1204 Germantown Avenue.
No. 2, June 10, Touro Hall, Tenth and Carpenter streets.
No. 3, June 17, 2856-58 Weikel street.

The room occupied by School No. 1 is wholly inadequate for the successful conduct of the work, it is the largest Hebrew School with the smallest floor space.

I would suggest that after the work in Touro Hall is completed, that arrangements be made for the purchase of two moderate sized houses, adjoining each other, and altered for purposes of your classes, as also for those of the Hebrew Sunday-School Society.

Miss Minnie Mayer donated a Bible which was awarded in School No. 1, as was also the Ulysses H. Rosskam prize and five dollar prize by Mrs. Florence K. Liveright.

The Norman and Courtney prizes were divided between Hebrew Schools Nos. 2 and 3.

NIGHT SCHOOL.

The Night School, which is open during the entire year, hardly gets the recognition it deserves, it is taken for granted that the classes are kept up to their standard, pupils come and go and teachers perform their duties satisfactorily. Those who leave the School, having obtained as much as they could receive or acquire, sever their connections entirely and are rarely again heard of; no trace of them is possible, although most of those who were in the Segar and Garment Making and Cutting classes are known to have obtained employment.

MOSES H. LICHTEN
Board of Officers, 1892–1893.

Typewriting and Stenography is a recent branch of instruction, hence but little can be said as to its results.

Commencement exercises of the Night School were held Thursday evening, June 30.

There were present of the Board: Benjamin Wolf, President; Ephraim Lederer, Vice-President; Henry M. Frank, Chairman of the Industrial Committee, and D. Sulzberger, Secretary.

MORTON M. NEWBURGER.

Mr. Isaac Husik, instructor in Hebrew in Gratz College, delivered the opening address.

Misses Corinne B. Arnold and Beulah Brylawski and

Ephraim Lederer, Esq., acted as judges to award the Isidore Coons prize for the best recitation, which was awarded to Samuel Lazowick, Solomon Aaronchik and John Posner, the Committee deciding that there was sufficient merit in each of the recitations to entitle the above named to a portion of the prize.

The Gabriel Blum Prize (The Jewish Year), was awarded to Barnet Ginvert for general progress.

Mr. Wolf presented the diplomas to the seventeen graduates, and the prizes to the pupils of the various classes.

Mr. Ephraim Lederer delivered the closing address to the graduates.

The exercises were concluded with the

EPHRAIM LEDERER
Board of Officers, 1887—1898
Vice-President 1896——

Star Spangled Banner being sung by the audience. Miss Emma Brylawski kindly performed the piano accompaniment.

From March 17 to June 16, Mr. Lederer delivered a course of ten lectures on the Constitution of the United States.

The nativity of the 1074 pupils admitted was as follows:

Russia, 777; United States, 116; Austria, 73; Roumania, 29; Germany, 30; Italy, 16; England, 15; Cuba, 6; Belgium, 4; Turkey, 2; France, 2; Bulgaria, 1; Canada, 1; Greece, 1; Palestine, 1.

Port of Arrival: New York, 403; Philadelphia, 476; Baltimore, 70; Boston, 3; St. Johns, 2; Portland, 1; Halifax, 1; Quebec, 1; Tampa, 1.

JOSEPH J. SNELLENBURG
Board of Officers, 1882-1895

SEWING SCHOOL.

On July 5, 1898, a sewing school was opened in Touro Hall under the joint charge of the Jewish Women's Council and the Young Women's Union, and discontinued September 1.

On January 8, 1899, the following communication was received from Mrs. Isaac Gimbel:

1541 N. 16th St.,
PHILADELPHIA, January 7, 1899.

To the Board of Officers of the Hebrew Education Society:

LADIES AND GENTLEMEN:—Finding there is a need of another school in the southern section of the city, and being desirous of opening such a school, but not having sufficient means to pay a superintendent, we, the Council of Jewish Women, would be willing to undertake the entire control of the school if you could supply the funds for paying one teacher. The one which was carried on during the summer in your Hall under the auspices of the Council did so much good work, that we would greatly regret that the lack of sufficient means would compel us to discon-

MORRIS SICKLES

tinue so good a work. Trusting the proposition will meet with your approval.

I am yours, etc.,

RACHEL F. GIMBEL,

Chairman of Sewing School Committee, Council of Jewish Women.

The Board took favorable action and the school opened, the attendance averaging 70 daily. it became necessary to employ an assistant.

The Dressmaking Class in which is taught drafting, cutting and fitting, and sewing by hand and machine, and the Millinery Class in which instruction is given in making frames, covering hats with straw,

BENJAMIN WOLF
Board of Officers, 1894—1895
Vice President, 1896—1898
President, 1898——

silk, velvet and other material, are all that could be desired; and the ladies of the Board, in whose charge these branches are, are enthusiastic in their praise of the instructors and their methods, but the attendance in these classes is not as large as it should be.

FREE SYNAGOGUE.

Religious services on Rosh-ha-Shanah and Kippur has become an established fact, this year being under the management of the instructors of the Night School aided by some of the pupils of the School; the thanks of the Society are due to Messrs. Bernard Harris, Samuel Israeli George Goward and L. Schwerin for their successful efforts to have the services properly conducted, though it can be positively stated that none more orderly or impresive was held in the city.

SAMUEL M. HYNEMAN
Board of Officers, 1894—

The cost which was but nominal, was paid by a few ladies and gentlemen who have contributed the requisite amount each year, their names will be found in the Treasurer's Report.

BATHS.

The Board after mature deliberation has decided to recommend the removal of the swimming-pool, owing to the fact that the water cannot change fast enough for the immense number of bathers using the pool during the summer months; from one hundred and fifty to two hundred in one hour, is too great a number to bathe in water which cannot possibly change entire in less than three hours. Eleven shower baths are now in operation, and the Board of Officers suggest that twelve more be built as soon as means are at hand for the purpose, plans having already been prepared by the architects.

HENRY M. FRANK
Board of Officers, 1895—

On the fifteenth of June, 1898, the swimming pool was

HEBREW EDUCATION SOCIETY.

opened, it was visited by 1500 bathers in June, 8800 bathers in July, and in August by 9300.

HEBREW SUNDAY SCHOOL.

The Hebrew Sunday School Society occupies the building for its School on Sunday morning and afternoon; in the morning for its Religious School and in the afternoon by its Sewing School; while on this subject I would call the attention of the public to the work done by this Society.

It has now in operation the Northern School, Third and Germantown avenue, 865 pupils; the Southern School at Touro Hall, Tenth and Carpenter streets, with 1076 pupils;

SIDNEY TRIESTE

South-Eastern School at Washington Hall, Fourth and South streets, with 675 pupils, and the School at Columbia Hall, Eight and South streets, with 487 pupils, making a total of 3103 pupils.

B'NAI B'RITH MANUAL TRAINING SCHOOL.

The technical school under the auspices of the Independent Order B'nai B'rith is doing good work, the pupils are being taught mechanical drawing, joining, carpentering, etc.; the instructors, Messrs. Hetzell and Alker, are thoroughly conversant with the latest methods adopted in the Public Manual Training Schools; Mr. Alker being instructor in joinery in the Central Manual Training School of this city.

GRATZ COLLEGE.

The classes of the Gratz College still hold their sessions in Touro Hall, where three rooms are set apart for their uses.

JOSEPH ROSENBAUM.

BARON DE HIRSCH COMMITTEE.

The Baron De Hirsch Committee still occupies the office room of which it has been in possession for several years past.

The office is open each morning and afternoon when Mr. George Goward, the superintendent, attends to the multifarious duties of his office, part of which, and not the least important, is the Employment Bureau.

ENTERTAINMENTS—TOURO HALL.

The following entertainments were held in Touro Hall:

April 27, 1898—Young Women's Branch of the Young Men's Hebrew Association.

July 2, 1898—Hebrew Sunday School, Punch and Judy Exhibition.

November 10, 1898—Touro Circle, composed of former pupils of the Hebrew Education Society's Night School.

December 11, 1898—Chanukah Entertainment of Hebrew Sunday School Society.

DAVID W. AMRAM,
Board of Officers 1896—

December 14, 1898—Manual Training School, B'nai B'rith.

Resolutions in regard to the deaths of Philip Lewin and Joseph J. Snellenburg were adopted at the meetings of the Board of Officers held May 8, and November 13, 1898, respectively, and were as follows:

"In common with all other charitable organizations of this city, the Hebrew Education Society of Philadelphia has suffered a grievous loss through the sudden demise of

PHILIP LEWIN,

who was for a long time an earnest co-laborer in the work of the Society, and for a number of years an active member of its Board of Officers.

In token of the high respect and esteem for the deceased by his surviving associates on the Board, it is ordered that the present minute be inscribed on the records of the Society."

BENJAMIN WOLF,
D. SULZBERGER, President.
Secretary.
Philadelphia, May 8, 1898.

Philadelphia, November 13, 1898.
Hebrew Education Society of Philadelphia.

The Board of Officers of this Society has learned with deep regret of the death of

JOSEPH J. SNELLENBURG.

He was for a number of years an active member of this Board, and aided materially in the educational work of the Society.

No call on him for assistance ever remained unanswered.

The Board of Officers tenders to the family its sincere sympathy in their bereavement.

BENJAMIN WOLF,
D. SULZBERGER, President.
Secretary.

DONATIONS.

The following donations were received during the year:

Report of Aguilar Free Library, New York.

Report of Smithsonian Institution (U. S. Nat. Museum), Washington, D. C., 1895.

Mrs. THERESA LOEB

Report of Smithsonian Institution (U. S. Nat. Museum), Washington, D. C., 1896.

Report of Bureau of Education, Washington, D. C.

14th Report of U. S. Civil Service Commission, July, 1896, to June, 1897.

14th Annual Report of Hebrew Technical Institute, 1898.

15th Year Catalogue of Hebrew Technical Institute, 1898.

John B. Alker, Catalogue of Central Manual Training School, 1898.

Hon. G. H. Gallinger, "Speech on Tariff."

Mrs. David Rosenheim, books and magazines.

The Misses Davidson, unbound books and magazines.

Mrs. Lena Frank, unbound books and magazines.

Lit Brothers, 500 America's National Songs.

Mrs. S. Kind, 29 books for Circulating Library.

Mr. Isaac Saller, one volume "Sadia Gaon."

Solomon Sulzberger, New York, "Menorah."

The Misses Phillips, magazines and Harper's Bazaars.

Horace A. Nathans, "History of England."

JOSEPH FELS
Board of Officers, 1885-1886

U. Z. Oberteuffer, six "Frank" series and one "Golden Treasury."

WILLIAM B. BOSSKAM
Board of Officers, 188—

B. H. Hartogensis, Jewish newspapers.

Miss Emily Phillips, two stereoscopes and views, books and calico and canton flannels.

Mrs. Chas. Follen Palmer, "Inebriety, its source, prevention and cure," by Charles Follen Palmer.

Mrs. Elvira N. Solis, New York, engraving the Origin of the Rites and Worship of the Hebrews.

Rev. D. Baruch, photograph of Judah Touro.

John B. Alker, library card box made by pupils of Manual Training School.

B'nai B'rith Manual Training School, gavel made by Benjamin S. Greenfield.

Mrs. Isaac Gimbel, treat to children of Sewing School.

Mrs. Felix Gerson, ten dolls for children of Sewing School who attended in the blizzard.

Benjamin Wolf, 1000 large envelopes and metal edge cards for signs in Touro Hall.

Mrs. Horace A. Nathans, six taper holders.

Mrs. Florence K. Liveright, five pair cutting plyers for Millinery Class.

Mrs. Florence K. Liveright, ten dollars to pay for exchanging a Wheeler & Wilson for a Domestic sewing machine.

Willimantic Linen Co., six dozen spools cotton for Sewing School.

Messrs. L. Bamberger & Co., two cases tobacco.

A legacy of one hundred dollars was received during the year from the Estate of Lucien Moss.

The following contributions have been received towards liquidating the mortgage of nine thousand dollars remaining on Touro Hall:

Isaac Rosskam	$500 00	A. M. Freehie	50 00
Louis Gerstley	500 00	Wm. B. Rosskam	50 00
Benj. Wolf	250 00	Max Levy	50 00
Gabriel Blum	250 00	Sam'l M. Hyneman	25 00
Moses A. Dropsie	250 00	Louis E. Levy	25 00
Jacob Muhr	250 00	Wm. B. Hackenburg	25 00
Edward Wolf	250 00	Ephraim Lederer	25 00
Mrs. Sarah Eisner	250 00	G. Rosenstein	3 00
Miss Emily Phillips	250 00	H. F. Bachman & Co.	250 00
Gimbel Brothers	150 00	Max Bamberger	250 00
Benj. W. Fleisher, Jr	150 00	Edward Loeb	100 00
Sam'l S. Fleisher	150 00	Mrs. Jane Friedenwald	50 00
Wm. Gerstley	100 00	Isidore Langsdorf	50 00
Maurice Bamberger	100 00	Herman Jonas	50 00
Andrew Kaas	100 00	Horace A. Nathans	50 00
Mrs. Eva Coons	100 00	August B. Loeb	25 00
Mrs. Florence K. Liveright	100 00	Henry M. Frank	25 00
Lit Brothers	100 00	A. M. Kohn	15 00

LIBRARY.

The Leeser Library has been used during the last year, but not to the extent that such a valuable collection would warrant. Every facility will be afforded to those who desire the use of the books, but circumstances have compelled the adoption of a rule which necessitates their use for reference only and in the building.

The Circulating Library has been largely patronized by the pupils of the Night School during the last few months. A number of books have been added to it, mainly juvenile.

The demand for books in Jargon having considerably increased, a number of them were recently purchased.

LIGHTING.

Before closing this report, I desire to mention that a question of importance has been considered by your Board of Officers, that of "Light."

The enormous sum of five hundred and forty-eight dollars and thirty cents was paid for gas (of this amount the fixtures and mantles cost seven dollars and thirty cents), and the bill for the present quarter, not included in this account, amounting to one hundred and sixty dollars.

Estimates have been obtained for installing an electric plant which would probably be no more expensive than the gas supply, and have the advantage of avoiding the intense heat thrown out by the gas lights during the summer months; the most rigid economy is practiced at all times, and your Board has hesitated to incur the expense of installation.

It will be noted by the report of the Treasurer that the list of members paying five dollars per annum has fallen off by twelve less paying this year, and the list of patrons paying twenty-five dollars by thirteen, causing a reduction from that source amounting to three hundred and eighty-five dollars; strenuous efforts should be made by every member of the Society, more especially by those composing the Board of Officers, to increase the membership.

Contributions for educational purposes is the highest and noblest kind of charity, for it tends to make our people better men and women and better citizens, instilling in them a love of race and love of country.

Respectfully submitted,

BENJAMIN WOLF,
President.

RESOLUTION

Adopted at the meeting of the Board of Officers on the occasion of the death of the Baroness Clara de Hirsch-Gereuth:

"In the death of the Baroness Clara de Hirsch-Gereuth, the Hebrew Education Society of Philadelphia, in common with the Jewish people throughout the world, bows in devout resignation to the Divine will.

"The broad philanthropy and the unstinted charity of the Baroness de Hirsch-Gereuth, attained a grandeur paralleled only by that of her equally lamented husband and affords an example of devotion to a high ideal which remains as a lustrous and imperishable memorial of her benificent life and as her most valuable heritage to the world which she blessed with her presence."

Treasurer's Report.

RECEIPTS.
From March 9, 1898 to March 12, 1899.

Baron de Hirsch Fund	$2,400 00
239 Members	1,195 00
68 Patrons	1,700 00
11 Friends	1,100 00
Interest on Mortgages and Deposits	1,155 37
Hebrew Charity Ball 1898	508 00
Miss Emily Phillips	200 00
Hon. Mayer Sulzberger	100 00
Chevra Thillim	25 00
Henry Jonas	5 00
H. A. Nathans (Norman & Courtney Prize)	10 00
Isaac Rosskam (Ulysses H. Rosskam Prize)	10 00
Books	10 88
Cigars	292 00

FREE SYNAGOGUE ACCOUNT.

Rosskam, Gerstley & Co.	$15 00	
Benjamin Wolf	10 00	
Miss Emily Phillips	10 00	
Wm. B. Hackenburg	5 00	
Hon. Mayer Sulzberger	5 00	
Horace A. Nathans	5 00	
Ludwig Leberman	5 00	
Benj. W. Fleisher, Jr.	5 00	
Mrs. Eva Coons	5 00	
Mrs. Florence K. Liveright	5 00	
Mrs. Jane Friedenwald	5 00	
Edward Wolf	5 00	
Mrs. Abr. S. Wolf	2 00	
Mrs. H. S. Louchheim	2 00	
	84 00	
		$8,787 25

EXPENDITURES.

Teachers' Salaries	Night School	$1,120 50	
"	" Industrial "	1,642 85	
"	" Hebrew "	900 00	
			$3,663 35

Janitor's Salary	$813 75	
Librarian's "	162 00	
Collector	77 50	
		1,053 00
Gas	$541 00	
Mantles	7 30	
	$548 30	
Coal	240 15	
Interest on Mortgage	467 55	
Rent	100 00	
Insurance	99 80	
Water Tax	43 20	
		1,499 00

INDUSTRIAL.

Tobacco	$117 63	
Revenue (Cigar) Stamps	91 20	
Cigar Boxes	41 00	
	$249 83	
Sundry Supplies	58 23	
		308 06

GENERAL SUPPLIES.

Stationary	$74 20	
Hebrew Books	57 09	
English "	68 33	
Library "	26 41	
Sundry Supplies	25 86	
		251 89
Annual Reports	$55 00	
Distributing	5 00	
	$60 00	
Fire-Proof Safe	45 00	
Clerical Work	20 00	
		125 00

FREE SYNAGOGUE.

For Expense in Carrying on Service	84 00

GENERAL EXPENSE.

Additional Coal-bin	$105 00	
Carpenter Work	$75 91	
Lumber	18 75	
		94 66
Plumbing and Steam Fitting	71 45	

Glazing	6.82	
Painting	10.00	
Bricklaying	1.50	
Stamped Envelopes and Postage	17.90	
Engrossing and Frames	22.22	
Examination Expense	17.28	
Advertising	22.50	
Printing	17.25	
Hauling Ashes	18.75	
Book-binding	4.00	
Repairing machine and hardware	4.41	
Collateral Inheritance Tax	5.00	
Petty Cash	64.37	
		526.11
		7,510.66
Deficiency, 1898		784.84
Total		$8,295.50

Receipts	$8,787.25	
Expenditures	8,295.50	
	$491.75	
Deduct 10 per cent. from Income	878.72	
Leaves deficit		$386.97

SPECIAL FUND.

Balance on hand March 8, 1898	$4,360.76	
Five per cent. Collateral Inheritance Tax (Est. M. Sickels)	5.00	
Ten per cent. General Fund, 1898	890.57	
Lucien Moss (Legacy)	100.00	
Mortgage paid (4th and Wood Streets)	5,019.25	
Interest on Deposit	85.53	
		$10,961.11

SUBSCRIPTIONS PAID ON MORTGAGE FUND.

Miss Emily Phillips	$250.00	
A. M. Frechie	50.00	
Wm. B. Hackenburg	25.00	
G. Rosenstein	3.00	
		328.00
		$11,289.11
Purchase of Mortgage (N. W. cor. 56th and Market)		3,000.00
		$8,289.11

Ten per cent. of Income, 1898		$78 75
		$9,167 83
Belonging to Permanent Fund		5,157 00
		$3,992 83

BUILDING FUND.

Balance on hand, March, 1898	$978 98	
Interests on deposits	18 16	
		997 14

LIFE MEMBERS.

HONORARY LIFE MEMBERS OF BOARD OF OFFICERS.

Moses A. Dropsie, Esq.
Isaac Rosskam.

Sol. L. Levy, 138 S. 3d.
D. Sulzberger, 1220 N. 12th.
Mrs. B. F. Teller, 1727 Spring Garden.
Mrs. Dora Trieste, Washington, D. C.
Mrs. Abraham S. Wolf, 1530 Green St.

FRIENDS.

PAYING $100.00 PER ANNUM.

Coons, Mrs. Eva, 1510 Girard Ave.
Fleisher, B. W., 2301 Green.
Fleisher, Moyer, 2223 Green.
Gerstley, Louis, 1411 N. Broad.
Kaas, Andrew, 1430 N. 15th.
Muhr, Jacob, 1110 Chestnut.
Rosskam, Isaac, 1423 N. 15th.
Snellenburg, J. J., Estate.
Sternberger, Samuel, 2120 Spring Garden.
Wolf, Ed., 1323 N. Broad.

PATRONS.

PAYING $25.00 PER ANNUM.

Aloe, Sidney, 724 Market.
Arnold, Mrs. Minnie K., 4250 Parkside Ave.

Bamberger, L., 1438 N. Broad.
Bamberger, Max, 1711 Girard Ave.
Bamberger, Maurice, 1949 N. Broad.
Bamberger, Mrs. Maurice, 1949 N. Broad.
Bauer, Benj., S. E. cor. 13th and Market.
Blum, Gabriel, 1007 Market.

Blum, Mrs. Gabriel, Ogontz.
Blum, Ralph, 1007 Market.
Blumenthal, H. B., 48 N. 3d.

Dannenbaum, Morris, 808 Arch.
Dreifus, Maack, 1013 Market.

Eisner, Mrs. Z. L., 1231 N. Broad.
Espen, Mrs. Samuel, 2309 Green.

Fernberger, Henry, 1230 Market.
Fleisher, B. W., Jr., 28 S. 6th.

Fleisher, Louis, 513 Market.
Fleisher, S. S., 25th and Hamilton.
Fleisher, Simon B., 2220 Green.
Frank, Henry M., 2349 Park Ave.
Frank, Mrs. Rosa, 2224 Green.
Frank, Jacob S., 2023 Spring Garden.
Freehie, A. M., 1529 N. 7th.
Friedenwald, Mrs. Jane, 915 N. 16th.

Gerstley, Wm., 1409 N. Broad.
Gimbel, Chas., S. E. cor. 9th and Market.
Gimbel, Ellis A., S. E. cor. 9th and Market.
Greenwald, Joseph L., 601 Chestnut.

Hackenburg, Mrs. Wm. B., 953 N. 8th.

Jonas, Herman, 1007 Market.

Katzenberg, L., 1345 N. 12th.
Kohn, Samuel, 722 Market.
Kohn, Simon L., 722 Market.
Kirschbaum, Simon, 724 Market.

Langsdorf, Isidore, 317 N. 7th.
Lit, Jacob D., N. E. cor. 8th and Market.
Lit, Samuel D., N. E. cor. 8th and Market.
Liveright, Max, 1418 Girard Ave.
Liveright, Mrs. Florence K., 910 N. Broad.
Loeb, August B., 2124 Spring Garden.
Loeb, Mrs. Marx B., 1321 Franklin.
Louchheim, Mrs. H. S., 949 N. 16th.
Louchheim, Joseph A., 2134 Green.

Marks, Emanuel, 8th and Arch.
Marks, Ferdinand, 8th and Arch.
Marks, William, 8th and Arch.
Muhr, Mrs. Fanny, 909 N. Broad.
Myers, Angelo, 1823 Spring Garden.

Nathans, Mrs. H. A., 1500 Centennial Ave.
Nirdlinger, Samuel, 842 N. Broad.

Pfaelzer, Morris, 1524 N. 16th.
Pfaelzer, Simon, 1430 N. 16th.

Rosenbaum, Henry M., 1421 Poplar.
Rothschild, Henry, 1220 N. 7th.

Selig, Eli K., 724 Market.
Snellenburg, Nathan, 12th and Market.
Snellenburg, Samuel, 12th and Market.
Snellenburg, Mrs. Samuel, 2127 N. Broad.
Solomons, A. A., 121 Walnut.
Steinbach, Dr. L. W., 1309 N. Broad.
Steppacher, Walter M., 2028 Wallace.
Strouse, Mrs. Levi, 722 N. 7th.

Teller, Frank, 1816 Girard Ave.
Teller, Joseph R., 1518 Fairmount Ave.

Wolf, Albert, 508 Minor.
Wolf, Benj., 621 Cherry.
Wolf, Mrs. Benj., 1506 Girard Ave.
Wolf, Clarence, 508 Minor.
Wolf, Mrs. Clarence, 910 Franklin.
Wolf, Edwin, 1619 Poplar.
Wolf, Frank, Franklin and Vine.
Wolf, Isaac, Jr., Franklin and Vine.

MEMBERS.

PAYING $5.00 PER ANNUM.

Abeles, Simon, 806 N. 7th.
Adler, Mrs. Abr., 2223 Green.
Adler, Dr. Cyrus, Smithsonian Institution, Washington, D. C.
Amram, D. W., 605 Chestnut St.
Appel, Alex M., N. E. cor. 10th and Filbert.
Arnold, Miss Julia, 645 N. 22d.
Arnold, Philip, 2113 Spring Garden.

Bachman, Frank H., 121 S. 5th.
Bamberger, Mrs. Fannie, 1319 N. 19th.
Bamberger, Wm., 1438 N. Broad.
Baum, Nathan, 223 N. 3d.
Belmont, Mrs. Max, 1515 Fairmount Ave.
Benswanger, Mrs. E., 1624 Diamond.
Bernheimer, Morris, 904 Richmond.
Berkowitz, Rev. Dr. Henry, 1529 N. 33d.
Birnbaum, Mrs M., 1733 N. 17th.
Blumenthal, Sol., 48 N. Third.
Brandes, Mrs. J.
Brunswick, R., 2251 N. Broad.
Burnstine, Alexander, 2055 E. Cambria.
Burnstein, J. L., 2340 N. Front.

Cohen, Charles J., 334 S. 21st.
Cohen, Samuel.
Cohen, Dr. S. Solis, 219 S. 17th.

Daniels, Gus., 2022 Wallace
Dannenbaum, Mrs. H., 2013 Spring Garden.
Dannenbaum, Ed. M., 2013 Spring Garden.
Dessauer, Seligman, S. E. cor. 12th and Market.

Eichholz, Adolph, 2138 Gratz Ave.

Eliel, Mrs. Louis S., 1613 N. 15th.
Engel, J. M., 1212 N. 7th.
Eschner, Louis, 2004 Park Ave.
Eschner, Mrs. L., 2004 Park Ave.
Espen, Jacob, 1020 Chestnut.
Espen, Samuel, 2309 Green.

Fels, Joseph, 1710 Market.
Fels, Morris, 1312 Franklin.
Fels, Samuel S., 1710 Market.
Feustman, Mrs. B. H., 1512 Girard Ave.
Fleisher, Mrs. Alex., 1955 Wallace.
Fleisher, Mrs. B. W., Jr., 1736 Spring Garden.
Fleisher, Miss Helen, 2220 Green.
Fleisher, Henry, 513 Market.
Fleisher, Mrs. Moyer, 2223 Green.
Fleisher, Penrose, 1910 Spring Garden.
Fleisher, Mrs. Simon, 2030 Green.
Fleishman, Rev. S. M., Jewish Foster Home.
Frank, Leopold, 1007 Market.
Frank, Martin, 7th and Cherry.
Frank, Mayer, 961 Franklin.
Frechie, Mayer S., 1336 N. 6th.
Freedman, Chas., S. E. cor. 7th and Cherry.
Friedman, H. S., 1422 N. 16th.
Friedenwald, Dr. Herbert, Library of Congress, Washington, D. C.

Gans, Mrs. Aaron, 2020 Green.
Gerstley, Mrs. Wm., 1409 N. Broad.
Gimbel, Ben., 9th and Market.
Goldbacher, R., 1927 N. 8th.
Goldstein, Mrs. Jacob, 1414 N. 16th.
Greenewald, B. F., 1015 Market.
Greenwald, Mrs. D., 2417 Master.
Greenwald, David, 9 N. 3d.
Greenwald, Samuel, 9 N. 3d.

Haas, S. L., 1703 Franklin.
Hackenburg, Wm. B., 516 Market.
Hagedorn, J. J., 946 Franklin.
Harris, Bernard, 209 South 6th.
Hecht, Samuel, 1103 Chestnut.
Heller, Mrs. Herman, 934 Franklin.
Henly, Jacob, 831 Arch.
Hess, Mrs. Henry, 1632 Franklin.
Hirsh, Alfred C., 1518 Jefferson.
Hirsh, Henry, 1418 N. 16th.
Hirsh, Wm. M., 1431 N. 15th.
Hirshler, Moses, 1310 Franklin.
Hyneman, Jacob E., 418 Walnut.
Hyneman, Samuel M., S. E. cor. Broad and Chestnut.

Jastrow, Dr. M., Jr., Univ. of Pa.
Jastrow, Rev. Dr. M., 139 W. Upsal, Germantown.
Jeitles, H. A., 865 Randolph.
Jonas, Mrs. Henry, 1847 Park Ave.
Jurist, Mrs. Louis, 916 N. Broad.

Katz, Marcus, 925 Franklin.
Katzenberg, Mrs. L., 1345 N. 12th.
Kahn, Samuel, 1420 S. Penn Sq.
Kauffman, Eugene, 137 N. 7th.
Kaufman, M. A., 137 N. 7th.
Kaufman, Mrs. J., 1325 Franklin.
Kind, Samuel, 1515 N. 10th.
Kirschbaum, Mrs. A. B., 1315 N. Broad.
Kirschbaum, Bernard, 1315 N. Broad.
Kohn, Abr., M., 910 N. 6th.
Kohn, Simon, 41 N. 3d.
Krieger, Jacob, 1320 Brown.
Krieger, Mrs. S., 1814 N. 18th.

Labe, Ben., 1231 N. 7th.
Labe, Mrs. Ben., 1231 N. 7th.
Lang, Isaac M., 1822 N. 7th.
Lang, Mrs. Morris, 2240 N. Broad.
Langfeld, A. M., N. W. cor. 10th and Filbert.
Langfeld, Isaac, 1319 N. 7th.
Langfeld, M. F., 2117 Master.
Langsdorf, Mrs. M. K., 724 N. 6th.
Leberman, L., 722 Franklin.

Leberman, Mrs. L., 722 Franklin.
Lederer, Ephraim, 1001 Chestnut.
Lemberg, E., 1446 Frankford Ave.
Leopold, Mrs. Isaac, 1520 Franklin.
Levi, Moses, 409 S. 9th.
Levinthal, Rabbi B. L., 534 Pine
Levy, Louis E., 854 N. 8th.
Levy, Max, 1213 Race.
Lichten, Moses, 1853 Park Ave.
Lichten, Wm., 12th and Washington Ave.
Linse, Sol., 626 South.
Lipper, M. W., 1518 Girard Ave.
Liveright, Morris, 1742 Franklin.
Loeb, Arthur, cor. Columbia and Germantown Aves.
Loeb, Herman, N. W. cor. 4th and Race.
Loeb, Horace.
Loeb, Horace, 51 N. 3d.
Loeb, Jacob F., 51 N. 3d.
Loeb, Leo, 929 N. 8th.
Loeb, Mrs. Leo, 929 N. 8th.
Loeb, Leopold, 306 N. 3d.
Loeb, Solomon, 306 N. 3d.
Loeb, Simon, 1508 Girard Ave.
Louchheim, Mrs. Jos., 715 N. 6th.
Louer, Mrs. L., 2113 Spring Garden.
Lowenstein, B., 805 N. 8th.

Massman, Mrs. A. E., 1511 N. 15th.
Mastbaum, Levi, 1332 Franklin.
May, Mrs. S., 719 Brown.
Mayer, Clinton O., 601 Chestnut.
Mayer, Levi, 826 N. 7th.
Mayer, Marx S., 411 Walnut.
Merz, Daniel, 704 N. 5th.
Miller, Jacob, 1521 N. 8th.
Miller, Simon, 926 Market.
Miller, Wm. W., 926 Market.
Morris, Wm., 702 Chestnut.
Morwitz, Joseph, 614 Chestnut.
Myers, Jos., 2308 Green.
Myers, Nathan L., 226 S. Front.

Nathans, H. A., 1500 Centennial Ave.
Nathanson, Harry, 12th and Market.

Netter, Mrs. Henry H., 951 N. 8th.
Netter, John, 2023 N. 19th.
Netter, Jos., 1820 Franklin.
Newburger, Alfred H., 714 Market.
Newburger, Morris, 2010 Green.
Newburger, Mrs. Morris, 2010 Green.

Pfaelzer, Mrs. Morris, 1524 N. 16th.
Pfaelzer, Mrs. Simon, 1430 N. 16th.
Powdermaker, Mrs. M., 839 N. 7th.

Rice, J. J., 1721 N. 15th.
Rosenau, Charles, cor. Columbia and Germantown Aves.
Rosenau, Nathan, 1903 N. 8th.
Rosenau, Philip, 1231 Susq. Ave.
Rosenberg, Morris, 716 Franklin.
Rosskam, Mrs. Isaac, 1423 N. 15th.
Rosskam, Joseph, 1423 N. 15th.
Rosskam, Wm. B., 1423 N. 15th.
Rothschild, Jacob, Cawker City, Kan.
Rothschild, Mrs. Henry, 1220 N. 7th.
Rothschild, Mrs. Sol., 1717 Jefferson.
Rubin, Mrs. Joseph H., 1623 N. 33d.

Sacks, Harry, 1223 Market.
Sacks, Samuel, 1223 Market.
Saller, Isaac, 2115 Spring Garden.
Saller, Mrs. Isaac, 2115 Spring Garden.
Saller, Louis, 2035 Spring Garden.
Schnitzer, H. M., 1007 Market.
Schwartz, Mrs. L., 1715 N. 18th.
Schwartz, M., 1336 N. 15th.
Seidenbach, Mrs. B., 1852 Park Ave.
Seidenbach, Mayer, 1709 Wallace.
Selig, Barney, 28 N. 3d.
Selig, Mrs. Sol., 2124 Spring Garden.
Shoneman, Louis, 116 N. 8th.
Shoyer, Saml. E., 1036 Arch.
Sichel, Julius, 1812 Mt. Vernon.
Silberman, Mrs. S., 1727 Spring Garden.
Snellenburg, Joseph N., 12th and Market.

Sondheim, Julius, 1231 N. Broad.
Springer, Emanuel, 1935 Wallace.
Steppacher, Mrs. Walter, 2028 Wallace.
Steppacher, Mrs. Wolf, 1730 Franklin.
Stern, C. K., 1409 N. 12th.
Stern, Edward, 112 N. 12th.
Stern, Harry F., Wilkesbarre, Pa.
Stern, Jacob, 428 N. 3d.
Stern, Mrs. M., 943 N. 8th.
Stern, M. H., 1609 Diamond.
Stern, Simon A., 836 N. 5th.
Strauss, Karl, 122 N. 3d.
Strauss, Samuel, 1845 N. 18th.
Strouse, Henry L., 837 Franklin.
Strouse, Nathan, 913 N. 16th.
Sulzberger, Joseph E., 1303 Girard Ave.
Sulzberger, Judge Mayer, 1303 Girard Ave.

Techner, Chas., 1611 N. 10th.
Teller, Benj. F., 1727 Spring Garden.
Teller, David, 903 N. 8th.
Teller, Jacob, 705 Corinthian Ave.
Teller, Louis E., 516 Market.
Teller, Louis, 1824 Girard Ave.
Teller, Oscar B., 606 Chestnut.
Teller, Raphael, 722 N. 6th.
Teller, Mrs. Solomon, 429 Green.
Teller, Dr. W. H., 2142 Green.
Troutman, M., 815 Franklin.

Uffenheimer, A. L., 115 N. 4th.

Van Beil, H., 927 N. Broad.
Vendig, Chas. H., 1922 N. 12th.

Wallerstein, David, Pelham, Mt. Airy.
Wedell, Mrs. R. P., 1410 N. Broad.
Weiller, Herman, 1352 Spring Garden.
Weinman, Joseph, 1702 Jefferson.
Weinman, Mrs. Joseph, 1702 Jefferson.

Weyl, Maurice. N. 112 N. 12th.
Wiener, George, 1912 N. 11th.
Wiener, Mrs. J., 866 N. 7th.
Wineland, Eli, 1435 Diamond.
Wineland, Mrs. Eli, 1435 Diamond.
Weiss, Mrs. J., 1726 N. 16th.
Wise, Mrs. August, 1514 N. 7th.
Wolf, Al., 910 Franklin.
Wolf, Mrs. D., 1308 N. 7th.

Wolf, Mrs. Edwin, 1610 Poplar.
Wolf, Elias, 314 N. 3d.
Wolf, Elias, 910 Franklin.
Wolf, Mrs. Elias, 910 Franklin.
Wolf, Mrs. Gus., 1733 Franklin.
Wolf, Gus., 1733 Franklin.
Wolf, Mrs. Herman, 826 N. 7th.
Wolf, Louis, 1529 N. 10th.
Wolf, Simon, 712 N. 7th.

www.ingramcontent.com/pod-product-compliance
Lightning Source LLC
Chambersburg PA
CBHW020925230426
43666CB00008B/1567